Social infrastruc
and left behind places

John Tomaney, Maeve Blackman, Lucy Natarajan,
Dimitrios Panayotopoulos-Tsiros,
Florence Sutcliffe-Braithwaite and Myfanwy Taylor

Regional Studies Policy Impact Books
Series Editor: Louise Kempton

LONDON AND NEW YORK

First published 2024
by Taylor & Francis
4 Park Square, Milton Park, Abingdon, Oxon, OX14 4RN

Taylor & Francis Group, an informa business

British Library Cataloguing-in-Publication Data
A catalogue record for this book is available from the British Library.

ISBN13: 978-1-032-71004-4 (print)
ISBN13: 978-1-032-71005-1 (e-book)

Typeset in 10.5/13.5 Myriad Pro
by Nova Techset Private Limited, Bengaluru and Chennai, India

Disclosure statement: No potential conflict of interest was reported by the authors.

The cover image was generated using the Midjourney AI software program. The Regional Studies Association hold a "Pro" licence subscription plan with Midjourney, valid at the time of first publication

Please visit https://taylorandfrancis.com/about/corporate-responsibility/accessibility-at-taylor-francis/ for further information on the accessibility features available for Regional Studies Policy Impact Books

CONTENTS

Social infrastructure and left behind places

Dedication

Augustine "Gus" Tomaney (1936–2022)

Pitman, faithful parishioner, son of Sacriston

"The memory of the righteous is a blessing" (Proverbs 10:7)

https://doi.org/10.1080/2578711X.2023.2254989

Acknowledgements

The research upon which this book is based was supported by UCL Grand Challenges, a UK Engineering and Physical Sciences Research Council (EPSRC) Impact Acceleration Award, and a project, "Beyond 'Left Behind' Places: Understanding Demographic and Socio-economic Change in Peripheral Regions in France, Germany and the UK", funded by the UK Economic and Social Research Council (ESRC), *L'Agence nationale de la recherche* (ANR) and *Deutsche Forschungsgemeinschaft* (DFG). Some of the ideas originated in an essay commissioned from John Tomaney by New Writing North for the Durham Book Festival in October 2017. We are grateful to Sarah Chaytor, Siobhan Morris, Katherine Welch and Julie Hipperson at UCL for their help in developing and managing the projects. The research was conducted in partnership with the Durham Miners' Association. Thanks to our collaborators in County Durham, especially Ross Forbes at the Durham Miners' Association, Heather Liddle at Sacriston Youth Project and Nathan Hopkins at Woodshed Workshop, Sacriston. Thanks also to Fiona Thompson at Framwellgate School, Durham. We are grateful to Stefan Noble and Kimberley Gregory at OCSI for permission to use the data reported in Figure 3.1. The ideas in this book were developed through discussions at: Regional Studies Association Conference, June 2021; JUC Public Administration Committee, Leicester, September 2021; Wales Institute of Social and Economic Research and Data, Cardiff, September 2021; Seoul National University, September 2021; University College London, October 2021; Hughes Hall, Cambridge, January 2022; Royal Geographical Society Annual Conference, Newcastle upon Tyne, August 2022; Centre for Urban and Regional Development Studies, Newcastle University, February 2023; and Regional Studies Association Policy Expo, May 2023. Thanks to Louise Kempton, series editor, for her support and close reading of the manuscript. For practical help, comments advice and/or helpful discussions, we thank especially Charlotte Carpenter, Estelle Evrard, Maurice Glasman, Rose Grayston, Patsy Healey, Victoria Hughes, Yunji Kim, Danny Mackinnon, Kevin Morgan, Jimin Oh, Emma Ormerod, Andy Pike, Jonathan Rutherford, Natasha Vall, Sanne Velthuis, Karel Williams and Jane Wills. Thanks also to Julian Harrop at Beamish Museum for help in sourcing photographs. The late Gus Tomaney knew more than most about Sacriston and pointed us in the right direction. This book is dedicated to his memory.

https://doi.org/10.1080/2578711X.2023.2254991

Foreword

Let behind places face many challenges and often struggle to find solutions. In *Social Infrastructure and Left Behind Places*, John Tomaney, Maeve Blackman, Lucy Natarajan, Dimitrios Panayotopoulos-Tsiros, Florence Sutcliffe-Braithwaite and Myfanwy Taylor confront these challenges and use them to make a call to action for governments at the regional, national and European levels to be more incisive in their development intervention.

Tomaney and his co-authors focus on the regions that have been excluded from the economic growth and prosperity enjoyed by dynamic areas, especially the bustling cities blending agglomeration and economic and political power. In their stead, left behind places have grappled with persistent poverty, economic decay and the crushing weight of missed opportunities.

Policymakers have, all too often, dismissed these places as inconsequential, fuelling a rising rebellion against the prevailing status quo—a phenomenon I have referred to as the rise and subsequent revenge of the "places that don't matter". But to dismiss them as irrelevant does not diminish their inherent economic potential. Not long ago, many left behind places were flourishing engines of growth and prosperity, and that potential still resides, latent, awaiting recognition and mobilisation. Yet, to unlock this potential there is a need, first, to acknowledge the problem and, then, to adopt more imaginative policy approaches catering to the unique needs of these communities. However, achieving success by policy intervention requires a deeper understanding of the challenges faced by these left behind areas.

Central to the book's exploration is an intensive study of one such place: Sacriston, a former mining village in County Durham, North East England. However, the methods, conclusions and policy implications of Sacriston's analysis resonate across left behind places not only in the UK and the rest of Europe but also beyond European borders.

As the authors contend, rebuilding social infrastructure in Sacriston—as in other neglected areas and regions—is a daunting task, yet not insurmountable. One that requires persistent

https://doi.org/10.1080/2578711X.2023.2254993

and consensual efforts aimed at both harnessing the power of belonging and collective memory, and at skilfully using productive nostalgia to instil hope and rekindle potential. In this respect, the book delves into a topic often overlooked: the realm of social infrastructure that remains relatively obscure, yet fundamentally vital. It holds the key not only to mobilising the dormant economic potential of declining regions but also to harmonising the policies implemented by various government tiers to bolster and contribute to overall development.

This ground-breaking book presents a compelling and much-needed addition to the debate on what to do with left behind places and how to promote development in areas that still have considerable hidden potential. This debate has been too frequently ignored as one that lacks sufficient allure, particularly when compared with the ubiquitous focus on superstar cities. Tomaney and his co-authors go to the root of the problem and recommend that rebuilding social infrastructure is fundamental to rejuvenating the economies of declining regions. They also posit that this task requires the involvement of all government tiers to implement policies that can contribute to their development and resurgence.

This is a timely and vital book, one that will undoubtedly spark many discussions and steer controversy. It will hold particular significance for researchers and policymakers alike, offering inspiration and guidance in addressing the often complex issues surrounding economic development. And, certainly, it will serve me well in my role as president of the High-Level Group on the Future of European Cohesion Policy,[1] as the reflections in the book are both opportune and deeply impactful for the majority of left behind areas in the European Union. The opinions versed in the book not only resonate with our ongoing deliberations but also present fresh perspectives on the potential and promise of social infrastructure for transforming the lives of countless communities.

Social Infrastructure and Left Behind Places represents a clarion call for change, a stirring tribute to hope and revitalisation, and a beacon guiding us towards a future where no place is left behind. A book that is more than just a simple academic endeavour, it offers hope for places that remain often forgotten, overlooked and neglected. We need to embrace this transformative vision for left behind areas, embarking on a journey that shall pave the way for more widespread prosperity and greater social cohesion across the UK, Europe and beyond.

Andrés Rodríguez-Pose
London School of Economics
President, High-Level Group
on the Future of European Cohesion Policy
A.Rodriguez-Pose@lse.ac.uk

NOTE

1 See https://ec.europa.eu/regional_policy/policy/how/future-cohesion-policy_en

 https://doi.org/10.1080/2578711X.2023.2254993

About the authors

John Tomaney is Professor of Urban and Regional Planning at University College London. His research interests are focused on the political economy of local and regional development. A Fellow of the UK Academy of Social Sciences and a Fellow of the Regional Studies Association, he is also a trustee of Redhills: the Durham Miners' Hall and Sacriston Youth Project. j.tomaney@ucl.ac.uk 0000-0002-7648-2910

Maeve Blackman worked as researcher with the Durham Miners' Association and is currently a senior research officer at Durham University and an associate lecturer at the Open University. She has worked extensively in the field of public engagement at the arts. She holds a PhD from Durham University. maeve@redhillsdurham.org.uk

Lucy Natarajan is Associate Professor in the Bartlett School of Planning at University College London. Her research centres on knowledge in community engagement and spatial planning. She is the co-editor of *Engaged Urban Pedagogy. Participatory Practices in Planning and Place-making* (UCL Press, 2023). lucy.natarajan@ucl.ac.uk 0000-0002-2855-4852

Dimitrios Panayotopoulos-Tsiros is a Research Associate and Lecturer at the Bartlett School of Planning, University College London, with a background in architecture and urban planning. His research centres on social and policy aspects of urban design. He has published in *Built Environment*, *Regional Studies* and *Urban Planning*. d.panayotopoulos@ucl.ac.uk 0000-0003-4101-9608

Florence Sutcliffe-Braithwaite is Associate Professor in Twentieth-Century British History at University College London. Her research focuses particularly on class, gender and politics. She is co-author of *Women and the Miners' Strike, 1984–1985* (Oxford University Press, 2023). f.sutcliffe-braithwaite@ucl.ac.uk 0000-0001-8114-6092

Myfanwy Taylor is Leverhulme Research Fellow in the Bartlett School of Planning, University College London. Her research focuses on urban economic development, planning and politics, especially collaborative research with grassroots group, and she has published in *International Journal of Urban and Regional Research*, *Area* and *Antipode*. She is a Trustee of West Green Road/Seven Sisters Development Trust in North London. myfanwy.taylor.09@ucl.ac.uk 0000-0003-2881-9192

Summary and recommendations

This book concerns the role of social infrastructure in "left behind places". The term "left behind places" refers to those towns and villages that have been excluded from the economic growth of past decades. Such places have attracted growing academic, political and policy attention, notably following events such as Brexit in the UK, the election of Donald Trump as President of the United States and *"Gilets Jaunes"* protests in France. Such events drew attention to a "geography of discontent" associated with grievances emanating from places beyond main metropolitan areas.

Similarly, there is growing academic and policy interest in the value of social infrastructure. Social infrastructure refers to the spaces in which people and communities gather and from which associational life—the coming together in common cause—grows. Recent analyses have emphasised the decline in social infrastructure and the extent to which this has undermined community cohesion. This is especially true of "left behind places" which, as we show, were once extraordinarily rich in social infrastructure, and the loss of which has been keenly felt.

This study has three objectives:

- To understand better the nature of "left behind places".
- To understand the process of making, unmaking and remaking of social infrastructure.
- To elicit policy recommendations.

Drawing on a range of international literature, we establish a framework for investigating the making, unmaking and remaking of social infrastructure in "left behind places". This recognises the importance of place attachments—the bonds that people feel toward where they live—which give rise to distinctive "moral communities". The making of social infrastructure is the result of local commitments and expresses local identity as well as meeting the material needs of people and communities. The unmaking of social infrastructure, especially where it

https://doi.org/10.1080/2578711X.2023.2254995

involves the ruination of the built environment, represents a form of "root shock" that disrupts place attachments. The production of stories about place is key to the formation "left behind places" as moral communities. In turn, stories provide the resources for the "radical hope" that underpins the (re)making of social infrastructure.

The book reports a "deep place study"—an intensive analysis drawing on a range of methods and working with local people and organisations—designed to explore the material and affective aspects of life in one village. We examine a former coal mining community, Sacriston, in North East England, where life changed when the colliery closed in 1985. This in-depth study allows us to provide a detailed account of the making, remaking and unmaking of social infrastructure. We demonstrate the need for immersion in the history and geography of place to enable an appropriate grasp of the factors at play in the (re) making of social infrastructure through time and space. Our methods for the study of social infrastructure and the framework we developed for understanding "left behind places" have wider applicability that extend beyond our single case. They are highly relevant to debates about "Levelling Up" in the UK. But, as Andrés Rodríguez-Pose notes in his preface to this book, the analysis and recommendations also have application for wider contemporary debates, such as the future of European Union (EU) Cohesion Policy. They speak to debates about, for instance, "*La France périphérique*", "*España Vaciada*", "Rustbelt America" or any place that experiences localised social and economic decline and the problems of being "left behind".

POLICY RECOMMENDATIONS

1. Social infrastructure is critical for social and economic well-being but it is hard to measure its benefits using traditional methods

Policymakers should guard against the unmaking of social infrastructure. Its loss can occur when policymakers look for quick solutions to strained public budgets, but the long-term consequences of its absence are now apparent. It affords a range of important overlapping, often intangible, benefits, which are difficult to quantify using conventional methods because such methods of value, for example, benefit–cost ratios, are poorly configured to measure it. The (re)makers of social infrastructure respond to perceived local needs rather than calculations of costs and benefits and (social) returns on investment. They are motivated by an ethic of care for their community, draw upon attachments to place and a sense of belonging, and enact shared values. It has hard to put a price on social infrastructure but it provides basic nourishment for communities. It should be seen as a component of the "foundational (or everyday) economy", that is, it concerns the basic requirements of civilised life in all communities, rather than contributing narrowly to "economic growth", "productivity" or "innovation".

Social infrastructure supports associational life that is a component of healthy democracies, and its absence is component of social and political polarisation.

2. The decline of social infrastructure is not a recent phenomenon, and its long history needs to be understood

Recent discussion has tended to link the decline of social infrastructure to the impact of austerity policies—notably in the UK since 2010—but we show that decline has been long-term process in "left behind places", linked to deindustrialisation and associated labour market changes, as well as changing retail, leisure and housing markets, shifting gender relations, etc.—indicating the scale of the challenge in its rebuilding.

3. Social infrastructure needs patient investment which provides funding for revenue as well as capital

Conventional investment appraisal approaches favour projects that generate quick and cheap returns in places where growth is strong. This undervalues the contribution of social infrastructure in "left behind places" whose returns are likely to be long term—perhaps generational—but can address problems such as loneliness, which have tangible health impacts that place heavy costs on already burdened medical systems. Public and private systems of investment appraisal need to reflect this. The (re)makers of social infrastructure have proved imaginative and adept at overcoming funding barriers, but it is easier to obtain finance for capital projects than revenue support. In the long-run revenue support is crucial to success.

4. Devolution of powers and decision-making to local actors is necessary for (re)building social infrastructure

In the UK, needs-based spending formulae, controlled centrally and targeted at places and projects that meet national criteria, neglect places where spending could be most impactful. Greater resource allocation to local government and local discretion in its allocation is a necessary requirement of a strategy for remaking social infrastructure. Competitive bidding processes often pitch local organisations against each other for government funding, duplicate efforts and waste scarce resources that could be better directed to the core objectives of social infrastructure providers. Philanthropy has filled in some of the gaps left by the withdrawal of the state and market, but it can reproduce some of the problems of the state: lack of long-term commitment, the imposition of top-down priorities, lack of transparency and accountability, and faulty valuation of costs and benefits.

5. Building social infrastructure is a long-term commitment

Social infrastructure takes a long time to build. It involves long-term commitments to place-making. The (re)making of social infrastructure cannot be legislated centrally but rests on sustained local action. Indeed, centralisation of policymaking is a cause of its decline. Devolved structures of government are a necessary but insufficient condition for the (re)making of social infrastructure. Local government should act as an enabler of community action, rather than substitute it. There are challenges here for university research. How do universities put their knowledge and expertise to work in "left-behind places"? How do they empower and enable the (re)makers of social infrastructure? For their research to make an impact in places that most need help, universities must commit to long-term investment in, and partnerships with, "left-behind places" that are not contingent on external grants or funding that tend to be for shorter timescales than needed to build genuine and effective collaboration.

6. Understanding the process and dynamics of social infrastructure building requires a range of methodological approaches

Our methods themselves are a key policy recommendation. The sustained immersion entailed in a "deep place" study demonstrates that building social infrastructure requires long-term commitments that harness the power of belonging and collective memory, and the use of productive nostalgia to instil hope and rekindle potential. Place, neighbourhood, communal cultures, stories and memory need to be rewritten into the politics and policy of social infrastructure because they are integral to the successful (re)making of social infrastructure.

7. A programme for social infrastructure

We call for a long-term financial commitment to a programme for the rebuilding of social infrastructure in "left behind places' that is led by local communities, but enabled by strategic intervention on the part of local, regional and national government, philanthropy and private actors, and anchor institutions such as universities. To yield its wider ranging and longer term benefits, rebuilding social infrastructure should be a central objective of local regeneration plans.

 https://doi.org/10.1080/2578711X.2023.2254995

1. Introduction

Keywords: left behind places; social infrastructure; regional policy; levelling up

This book is concerned with the role of social infrastructure in "left behind" places. The problem of "left behind" places has attracted growing political and policy attention internationally. The term "left behind", in many respects, lacks precision and is problematic insofar as it is pejorative and suggests a limiting judgement. But its currency arises from the role of "left behind" places in producing political shocks such as the election of Donald Trump, Brexit, the rise of Marine Le Pen and the Swedish Democrats, and the entry of Fratelli d'Italia into Italy's government. Andrés Rodríguez-Pose has theorised these moments as the "revenge of the places that do not matter",[1] manifesting a "geography of discontent".[2] These are places that have not shared in the growth and accumulation of wealth that has occurred in big cities and have become marked by multiple forms of social deprivation and deep political resentments. Many "left behind" places have long lagged average social and economic indicators despite being the target of waves of policy interventions, in some cases, over several decades. But recently "left behindness" has come to be seen not merely as a material condition, but also an affective one. The feeling of being "left behind" has both social and political implications, contributing to the rise of populist politics.

In the search for solutions for what seem like intractable problems, policymakers have begun to focus on the role of social infrastructure as an ingredient in the policy mix. Infrastructure provides the framework for social and economic development. It can be economic or social, hard or soft, tangible or intangible: it is relational.[3] Although imprecisely or inconsistently deployed in policy debates, Eric Klinenberg defines social infrastructure as "the physical places and organisations that shape the way people interact".[4] He defines social infrastructure "capaciously" to include "libraries, schools, playgrounds, parks, athletics fields and swimming pools", as well as "sidewalks, courtyards, community gardens, and other green spaces that invite people into the public realm". He also counts "community organisations, including churches and civic associations" and "regularly scheduled markets" that allow people to assemble.[5] For others, social infrastructure also embodies the activities that occur within physical places.

Social infrastructure has begun to appear in policy repertoires in several countries. Responding to growing concern about the decline of "Regional Australia",[6] Infrastructure Australia identified "regional opportunities and gaps" in infrastructure provision in non-metropolitan areas. Specifically, it called for improvements in social infrastructure but left the concept undefined.[7] President Joe Biden's "American Jobs Plan" made provision for the remediation and redevelopment of "idle real property, and spur the buildout of critical physical, social, and civic infrastructure in distressed and disadvantaged communities".[8] Again, this is largely undefined but focuses on care support for children and the elderly. Moreover, Klinenberg suggests Biden's plans are too focused on investments in physical capital and insufficiently attentive to social infrastructure.[9] By contrast, in France, responding to the grievances raises by the "*Gilets Jaunes*" protesters and broader discontent in "peripheral France",[10] the *Ministère de la Transition écologique et de la Cohésion des territoires* (Ministry for Ecological Transition and Territorial Cohesion) has developed a programme aimed at helping local efforts to overcome social isolation, recognising

https://doi.org/10.1080/2578711X.2023.2254996

that citizens have been creating "third places" ("*tiers-lieux*") in order to rebuild social ties.[11] In Germany, the *Bundesministerium des Innern und für Bau und Heimat's "Soziale Stadt"* programme provided resources for social infrastructure "*sozialen Infrastrukturen*" provision, with a focus on disadvantaged neighbourhoods.[12] The European Commission has also demonstrated a concern with the need to fix deficits in social infrastructure provision.[13]

1.1 SOCIAL INFRASTRUCTURE AND "LEVELLING UP" IN THE UK

In the UK context, recent policy toward left behind places has been framed through the lens of "levelling up",[14] a policy which received its fullest presentation in the UK government's White Paper *Levelling Up the United Kingdom*.[15] The principal authors of the White Paper claim that "levelling up" is a part economic, part social, part moral mission "to unleash opportunity, prosperity and pride in places where, for too long, it has been held back".[16] For the-then prime minister, Boris Johnson, specifically it concerns investing in "areas that have for too long felt left behind".[17] "Social infrastructure" is referred to 10 times in 300 plus pages of the "Levelling Up" White Paper, although it is never defined, nor used consistently. (By contrast, the terms "ambition" or "ambitious" are used 69 times.) Curiously, social infrastructure is conceived in terms of how in contributes economic agglomeration, despite the little of the literature on topic making this link. For example:

> Social capital and social infrastructure amplify the forces of economic agglomeration. Good housing, high streets, and leisure and cultural activities serve as a magnet for skilled people, meaning those places continue to steam ahead. Historically, culture and creativity were at the heart of the Medici effect. So it is in many of today's global super-cities.[18]

The dominant concern with agglomeration means that much of the White Paper focuses on conventional approaches to regional policy, such investment in physical infrastructure, research and development (R&D) and raising gross value added (GVA), although it is not made clear how this will assist "left behind" places. It is implied that the lack of social infrastructure contributes to left behindness, although the reasoning for this conclusion is unclear. But the decline of social infrastructure is considered a component of self-fulfilling negative "social narratives" that drive behaviour, and economic and financial decisions. Akin to Leo Tolstoy's dictum that "Happy families are all alike; every unhappy family is unhappy in its own way",[19] the White Paper acknowledges that while success looks similar everywhere—the presence of factors that underpin economic agglomeration—the opposite is the case for "left behind" places.

For left behind places, the picture is more complex. Depletions or deficiencies in physical, human, intangible, financial, social or institutional capitals can have knock-on effects to the

https://doi.org/10.1080/2578711X.2023.2254996

other capitals in a self-enforcing, vicious spiral of low income and weak growth. Many "left behind places" are weak in different ways, with a complex and interacting mix of economic, financial and social problems.[20] The White Paper calls for a focus on "local communities and social infrastructure" and "the role of neighbourhood policies and strategies for building community capacity in left behind areas"[21] and makes one of its targets the restoration of "a sense of community, local pride and belonging, especially in those places where they have been lost".[22]

The White Paper proffers "stronger pride in place" as the intended outcome of these efforts, but this objective is weakly defined. The approach outlined in the White Paper owes much to Rachel Wolf, author of the 2019 Conservative Manifesto, who identified the need for, what she termed, "levers and tests" to guide levelling up, in effect, central government funds aimed at local communities.[23] Wolf states:

> If the government wants to show it really understands people and places, it is going to need to use its vast plethora of funds—the leveling up fund (sic), the towns fund, the safer streets fund—to invest in the physical fabric of places, and in supporting shops, events, and culture. Bluntly, it needs hanging baskets: the "small stuff" that sounds boring in a speech, but actually matters to people and gives them renewed pride in where they live.[24]

In the Levelling Up White Paper, this translates into centrally determined "Pride in Place" targets.

> By 2030, pride in place, such as people's satisfaction with their town centre and engagement in local culture and community, will have risen in every area of the UK, with the gap between top performing and other areas closing.[25]

In this book we show how these policies aimed at improving "pride in place" offer a thin and impoverished version of place-making, at odds, in fact, with the White Paper's own analysis that "left behind" places are complex and diverse. The White Paper demonstrates little grasp of the factors behind the making, unmaking and remaking of social infrastructure and the role it plays in communities: hanging baskets are unlikely to be the answer. In summer 2023, the UK government had yet to propose measures for improving "pride in place", or a mechanism for assessing the effectiveness of expenditure in pursuit of this objective. This task is likely to prove difficult because the way people feel about where they live is intrinsically difficult to measure. As we show in this book, measuring the non-economic aspects and benefits of social infrastructure is particularly difficult. Moreover, the notion that targets can be set centrally, levers pulled and outcomes achieved overlooks the importance of attachments, commitments and collective action in the production of social infrastructure. The White Paper suggests that "communities must have strong civic institutions, assets and relationships that anchor local pride in place",[26] but gives little indication of the long-term challenges involved in creating these. Overall, provisioning social infrastructure seems likely to be something done to communities rather than by communities. This may also be true of efforts to rebuild social infrastructure in other countries.[27]

1.2 STRUCTURE OF THE BOOK

While current UK policies toward "left behind places" are framed by the Levelling Up White Paper, our aim is to move beyond current policy fads and short-term fixes to develop a deeper account of how social infrastructure is made, unmade and remade, in order to inform a broader policy debate. We show that the making and remaking of social infrastructure is a long-term process that rests on myriad civic actions. In order do this we deploy methods that allow us to develop a deeper understanding of these processes. In particular, we pay attention to contemporary efforts to remake social infrastructure in unpropitious circumstances. Our aim is to develop a *deep place* understanding of social infrastructure-building. We achieve our objectives through a case study of the making, unmaking and remaking of social infrastructure in one village in North East England, Sacriston in County Durham. The solutions we propose for the development of social infrastructure in "left behind places" have been developed with our partners in the communities we have studied.

In chapter 2, we unpick the debate about "left behind" places, seeking to go beyond the view of them as bundles of social and economic indicators to see them, in the words of Robert Wuthnow, as "moral communities", and examine how the making of social infrastructure gives expression to this. Also, we review the emerging literature on social infrastructure, focusing especially on the claims it makes about the absence or loss of social infrastructure in "left behind" places. We use Mindy Fullilove's concept of "root shock" to describe the effects of this loss and identify and use Jonathan Lears' concept of "radical hope" to describe the conditions under which people act to remake social infrastructure. We arrive at these concepts inductively based on our understanding how social infrastructure is (re)made, arising from our ongoing relationship with our case study village and the social infrastructure builders whose commitments bring it into existence.

In chapter 3, reflecting our aim to develop a deep-place understanding, we set out our methodological approach to studying the making, unmaking and remaking of social infrastructure in "left behind" places. The aim is to develop a "deep place" study that can tell the story of change, rather than capture a moment or highlight a deficiency. We introduce our case study, Sacriston, the former coalmining village in County Durham. We suggest our methods are useful for offering a richer account of the factors that both produce social infrastructure and might bring it into crisis. Our methods involve developing close relationships with the actors in the village in order to understand their struggles and the nature of their achievements both historically and contemporaneously. We believe these methods as offering improved insights for policy.

In chapter 4, we briefly introduce our case study, Sacriston, a village whose life, from 1839 to 1985, was centred around a colliery, but in which people sought to form a community and build the social infrastructure that supported it. This context is vital for understanding the long-term process through which social infrastructure is made, unmade and remade.

In chapter 5, we describe the making of social infrastructure in Sacriston, showing how it gave expression to a particular moral community and the legacies bequeathed by these early efforts.

In Chapter 6, we describe the growing crisis of social infrastructure. We trace the long history of the unmaking of social infrastructure, but show how decline accelerated in recent decades to manifest in the form of "root shock". We map the scale of these losses. The destruction of key components of social infrastructure, symbolised by the closure of key buildings, feeds a sense of "left behindness".

In chapter 7, we report the herculean efforts of local people to remake social infrastructure in the most unpropitious circumstances in order meet community needs, seeing these efforts as examples of "radical hope". Our account emphasises the importance of local attachments and the commitments these affect among, at least some, members of the community dedicated to repairing the social fabric.

In chapter 8, we present our conclusions and policy recommendations. We note how successful social infrastructure affects the commitments of local people, often over generations. and cannot be legislated centrally. Local and central government cannot set targets and operate levers to create it, either in County Hall or Whitehall. Rather, the role of government shifts to one of *enabling* the flourishing of social infrastructure by respecting, listening to, resourcing and supporting locally embedded actors and organisations. The work of enabling itself holds the potential to stimulate further learning and policy innovation, transforming place-based development policy beyond the frame of social infrastructure. Our deep place study—and the methods we used to conduct it—are themselves modes of policy development that help to show how community actors identify needs but require time and resources to produce results.

NOTES

1 Rodríguez-Pose A (2018) The revenge of the places that don't matter (and what to do about it). *Cambridge Journal of Regions, Economy and Society*, 11(1): 189–209. https://doi.org/10.1093/cjres/rsx024

2 Dijkstra L, Poelman H and Rodríguez-Pose A (2019) The geography of EU discontent. *Regional Studies*, 54(6): 737–753. https://doi.org/10.1080/00343404.2019.1654603; McCann P and Ortega-Argilés R (2021) The UK "geography of discontent": Narratives, Brexit and inter-regional "levelling up". *Cambridge Journal of Regions, Economy and Society*, 14(3): 545–564. https://doi.org/10.1093/cjres/rsab017

3 Pike A, O'Brien P, Strickland T, Thrower T and Tomaney J (2019) *Financialising City Statecraft and Infrastructure*. Cheltenham: Edward Elgar. https://doi.org/10.4337/9781788118958

4 Klinenberg E (2020) *Palaces for People. How to Build a More Equal and United Society*. London: Vintage, at 5.

5 Klinenberg (2020), at 16, see Reference 4.

6 For instance, Chan G (2018) *Rusted Off. Why Country Australia is Fed Up*. North Sydney, NSW: Vintage; see also Tomaney J (2019) Book review: *Rusted Off: Why Country Australia is Fed Up* by Gabrielle Chan. *LSE Review of Books*, 11 June. https://blogs.lse.ac.uk/lsereviewofbooks/2019/06/11/book-review-rusted-off-why-country-australia-is-fed-up-by-gabrielle-chan/

7 Infrastructure Australia (2022) *Regional Strengths and Infrastructure Gaps*, at 39–40. https://www.infrastructureaustralia.gov.au/sites/default/files/2022-03/1_RSIG_Introduction_0.pdf

8 White House (2021) *Fact sheet: The American Jobs Plan*, 31 March. https://www.whitehouse.gov/briefing-room/statements-releases/2021/03/31/fact-sheet-the-american-jobs-plan/; see also Klinenberg E (2021) Infrastructure isn't really about roads. It's about the society we want. *New York Times*, 26 April. https://www.nytimes.com/2021/04/26/opinion/infrastructure-biden.html

9 Klinenberg (2021), see Reference 8.

10 Colomb C (2021) The revolt of the "periphery" against the "metropolis"? Making sense of the French Gilets Jaunes movement (2018–2020). *International Journal of Urban and Regional Research*. https://www.ijurr.org/spotlight-on/urban-revolts/the-revolt-of-the-periphery-against-the-metropolis/; see also Abboud L and Nolsøe E (2022) The corner of France that explains Macron, Le Pen and a deep political divide. *Financial Times*, 22 April. https://www.ft.com/content/5bd5e791-9561-42a0-ac8c-f5bdeeb81309

11 Ministère de la Transition écologique et de la Cohésion des territoires (2022) *Territoire*. 11 August. https://www.ecologie.gouv.fr/territoires

12 Bundesministerium des Innern und für Bau und Heimat (2018) *Programmstrategie Soziale Stadt*. https://www.bmi.bund.de/SharedDocs/downloads/DE/publikationen/themen/bauen/wohnen/programmstrategie-soziale-stadt.pdf?__blob=publicationFile&v=2

13 Fransen L, de Bufalo G and Reviiglio E (2018) *Boosting investment in social infrastructure in Europe* (European Economy Discussion Papers No. 2018/74). Brussels: Directorate-General for Economic and Social Affairs, European Commission. https://economy-finance.ec.europa.eu/publications/boosting-investment-social-infrastructure-europe_en

14 For some background on the politics of "levelling up" in the UK, see Tomaney J and Pike A (2020) Levelling up? *Political Quarterly*, 91(1): 43–48. https://doi.org/10.1111/1467-923X.12834

15 Department for Levelling Up, Housing and Communities (DLUHC) (2022) *Levelling Up the United Kingdom* (CP 604). https://www.gov.uk/government/publications/levelling-up-the-united-kingdom
16 DLUHC (2022), at x, see Reference 15.
17 DLUHC (2022), at viii, see Reference 15.
18 DLUHC (2022), at 46, see Reference 15.
19 Tolstoy L (1878/2014) *Anna Karenina*, trans. R Bartlett. Oxford: Oxford University Press, at 1.
20 DLUHC (2022), at 46, see Reference 15.
21 DLUHC (2022), at 247, see Reference 15.
22 DLUHC (2022), at 95, see Reference 15.
23 Wolf R (2021) Tests for the delivery of levelling up, and levers with which to deliver it. https://conservativehome.com/2021/05/10/rachel-wolf-tests-for-the-delivery-of-levelling-up-and-levers-with-which-deliver-it/
24 Wolf R (2020) Boris Johnson must sweat the small stuff to change lives post-Brexit. https://www.politico.eu/article/boris-johnson-must-sweat-the-small-stuff-to-change-lives-post-brexit/
25 DLUHC (2022), at 121, see Reference 15.
26 DLUHC (2022), at 205, see Reference 15.
27 Klinenberg (2021), see Reference 8.

2. "Left behind places" and social infrastructure

Keywords: left behind places; social infrastructure; place attachments; moral communities

2.1 INTRODUCTION

Originating in the UK and US, the term "left behind places" is being used more widely to describe the political economy of geographical inequalities. In this chapter, we unpack the key terms of the debate and explore the relationship between "left behindness" and the role played by deficiencies in social infrastructure as a prelude to our study of Sacriston.

A discourse on "left behind" places began to appear in politics and the media, especially after 2016, in the aftermath of the election of Donald Trump as US President and the Brexit referendum in the UK. It has gained wider currency since then, especially in political discourse, as a shorthand for widening geographical inequalities and associated political polarisation, following the Global Financial Crisis of 2008. Academic research is catching up with this political and popular discourse. A proliferation of studies has sought to quantify and explain geographical inequalities in the Global North and their apparent relationship with the appeal of populist politics in "left behind" places. Geographical inequalities are longstanding and have been subject to many efforts at amelioration.[1] Martin et al. have shown this especially true of the UK where the problems of lagging regions have been the focus of public policy since the 1960s.[2] The UK government's Levelling Up White Paper offers an explicit acceptance that past interventions have been ineffective, partly attributed to a failure to address the affective dimension of "left behindness". In many cases, what today are called "left behind places" have long lagged behind national averages of social and conditions, so recent research has asked what, if anything, is new about the current phase and whether there are different ways places are left behind and how this is experienced.[3]

Pike et al. suggest that the term "left behind places" modifies the ways in which geographical inequalities are interpreted and responded to, by highlighting the uneven effects of globalisation and economic restructuring, counterposed against the dynamism of "superstar" cities. Moreover, the term broadens interpretations beyond only economic issues to incorporate multiple, interrelated social, political, environmental and cultural dimensions. "Left behind" conditions are not solely economic in cause, expression or solution. Significantly, the term draws attention to the affective dimensions of "left behindness"; how people feel about where they live and the way these shapes lived experience, which can be expressed a sense of lost community.[4] It is these affective dimensions of "left behindness" that are the main focus here.

The role of social infrastructure in "left behind places" has merited particular attention because of its role in shaping the lived experience of communities. Once well provided, a growing body of research suggests that "left behind" places are comparatively underserved with respect to social infrastructure. Klinenberg maintains that, "As the factories shuttered, so too did the union halls, taverns, restaurants and civic organisations that glued different groups together".[5] The UK All Party Parliamentary Group on Left Behind Neighbourhoods suggests "left behind" places "have a social infrastructure deficit".[6] Local Trust, using data from OCSI, a

https://doi.org/10.1080/2578711X.2023.2254997

research company, has developed a Community Needs Index that proposes a tripartite typology featuring civic assets, community engagement and connectivity.[7] Deficiencies in social infrastructure map closely onto "left behind" places in the deindustrialised Northern regions and former seaside resorts in the UK.

Deficiencies in social infrastructure, then, contribute to a sense of "left behindness", as former centres of community activity disappear. In this chapter, then, we develop an inductive theoretical framework to explain the making, unmaking and remaking of social infrastructure in Sacriston, reflecting the "ethnographic sensibility" that guided our fieldwork (see chapter 3). Although our analytical focus is an English mining village, we draw on international literature to develop our framework of understanding, allowing us to develop a wider explanatory value and offer broad insights for policy. The material and the affective are connected but, by and large, the former has tended to receive most attention in academic and policy debates.

To fix this lacuna requires us to address questions of place attachment and belonging as they pertain to left behind places, which have only recently become the matter for political debate. Specifically, we address literature that highlights the ways communities can experience bereavement and loss in the face of disruptive social and economic change. This is most obvious with the closure of, say, a major employer that has provided not only jobs but also an identity for a community (e.g., "fishing village", "mill town", "slate valley", "seaside resort"). But a sense of loss can also arise when key facilities, which have been a focus of local life, such as a school or church, are closed. The emotional life of communities has intrinsic value, but it makes an instrumental contribution to the improvement of socio-economic conditions. We consider the emerging literature on social infrastructure in "left behind places", the role it plays and the consequences of its decline. We define social infrastructure as the locations in which belonging and attachment are produced and consider what this means when it is lost, especially in "left behind" places.

2.2 LEFT BEHIND

"Left behind places" is an increasingly used but loosely defined term—especially in the UK and US, but increasingly beyond—that foregrounds a political problem, invokes a geographical imaginary and animates policy debates.[8] But it risks simplifying and obscuring the complexity and diversity of problems and potentials in real places and can skew policy interventions in the wrong directions. Since 2008 and, especially, after 2016, it has come to refer to places beyond the major urban agglomerations that contain a disproportionate share of innovation, growth and wealth. Politically, "left behind places" are deemed to be overlooked by distant and self-interested metropolitan elites. The grievances of "left behind places" have been successfully mobilised electorally by populist forces to produce the "revenge of the places that do not matter".[9] Left behindness can exist across a range of socio-economic indicators, not all of which might be present in all "left behind places", partly explaining the proliferation of indexes that seek to quantify it.[10] But such aggregations run the risk of homogenising places and overlooking their distinctive qualities and the variegation among them.[11]

The frameworks for policy interventions in "left behind places" are hampered by the limits of our understanding of the nature of development in places.[12] Longstanding efforts focused on increasing gross domestic product (GDP) or gross value added (GVA); improving the performance of tradeable or export sector or promoting growth in "knowledge-intensive business services" in cities have failed to close the gaps with "left behind" places. The implication here is that people in there either await some of the proceeds of growth generated elsewhere or seek to access opportunities in faster growing places.[13] But people are not merely factors of production responding to market signals; they are also members of communities that affect belonging and attachments and are a focus for identities. A community, according to the poet Seamus Heaney, is "not simply a credit rating or an economy but a history and a culture, a human population rather than a statistical phenomenon".[14] According to Wuthnow, "left behind" places are founded on "moral communities"[15] that embody distinctive values that produce a strong attachments and sense of belonging.

We can see left behind places as a category of community. There are many types of community and even apparently homogenous communities contain division and conflict. But all communities have some things in common. They are constituted by the past and, thus, are "communities of memory", in the classic formulation of Bellah et al.[16] A constitutive narrative underpins the traditions of a community. Moreover, according to Wuthnow, "Small communities have stories about their history that help them make sense of their present."[17] In one reading, this is a recipe for an unproductive nostalgia. But nostalgia has useful psychological attributes: it generates positive affect, raises self-esteem, fosters social connections and alleviates perceived existential threats.[18] For Italian anthropologist Vito Teti, nostalgia can express both hope and remembrance and be mobilised in the invention of a new identities for communities.[19] A collective history, moreover, provides the foundations of "communities of hope" which connect current and individual efforts to larger common good. Memory and hope provide the frameworks in which ritual, aesthetic and ethical practices express a way of life. Such "practices of commitment" define "the patterns of loyalty and obligation that keep the community alive".[20] As Teti observes, communities are subject to constant change and "The only thing that remains are stories and with them the people who live to tell them".[21] Collective memory is crucial to the mobilisation of civic resources.[22] It is a social construction, shaped in part by the concerns of the present, and involves both continuity and change, forgetting and erasure as well as remembering. While it is individuals who remember, typically, they draw upon the social context to recollect and recreate the past. Hwalbachs maintains that it is in society that individuals recall, recognise and localise their memories.[23]

2.3 PLACE ATTACHMENTS

Communities enact attachments, but economic restructuring has led to the "destruction of belonging in our communities".[24] The French philosopher Simon Weil has written of the basic human need for roots and the costs of uprootedness.[25] The importance of place attachments—and the consequences of their disruption—has received attention in academic literature,[26] but has had comparatively little influence on the debate about "left behind" places. Attachments have a spatio-temporal dimension and a relational rather than a transactional character. Attachment theory considers the importance of connectedness between people in shaping patterns of human development.[27] In their comprehensive review of the literature on the importance of place attachment, especially from the viewpoint of environmental psychology, Manzo and Perkins conclude:

> Affective bond to place can help inspire action because people are motivated to seek, stay in, protect and improve places that are meaningful to them. Consequently, place attachment, place identity, and sense of community can provide a greater understanding of how neighborhood spaces can motivate ordinary residents to act collectively to preserve, protect or improve their community and participate in local planning processes.[28]

Damaged human attachments result in trauma, can arouse feelings of grief and create long-term psychological stress. The disruption of place attachments, however, can engender collective feelings of loss, akin to bereavement.[29] Mattison's research with voters in the Midlands and North of England attributed shifts in political attitudes to a sense of loss, typically resulting from the closure of a major employer which gives an identity to a place, such as the pottery industry in Stoke-on-Trent, in the English Midlands. Voters narrate the loss of local industry, and the society to which it gave rise, using the language of grief, while simultaneously expressing a sense of belonging partly derived from the identity produced by a distinctive industrial past.[30] Gömar has identified similar tenons in relation to former industrial towns in East Germany.[31] Research by Silver and colleagues for the Pew Research Center, based on focus groups in the US and UK, similarly ascribed feelings of being "left behind" to a "profound sense of loss".[32] Feelings of resentment arise from a sense of neglect and political abandonment.

For Wuthnow, in rural America, the closure of a major employer can induce within communities "a sense of loss, a feeling of grief".[33] Prendergast describes how men who lost their jobs following the closure of a 250-year-old paper mill in Watchet, Somerset, narrated their loss not in terms of economics but in terms of the value it gave to their lives.[34] So too can the closure of social infrastructure, such as a school. Such losses foment feelings of being left behind, even among households that can manage economically, or which have limited local connections:

> Being part of a moral community, even when it sits lightly on people's shoulders, means that sensing your community is declining and your young people are falling behind is a reflection in no small measure on you. You may not be affected personally, but you are part of a failing community.[35]

Personal attitudes, identity and perhaps even psychological characteristics are affected by community character, which is a product of local economic and social history. People and place are inescapably and inextricably connected. Abreu and Jones show that people in UK mining communities feel disenfranchised and ignored and are sceptical about political processes to a greater extent than elsewhere. Communal bonds are fraying. Apathy and cynicism, increased insularity, distrust and withdrawal from places and people "outside" mark these communities. Despite being the focus of policy and investment by various and changing development and regeneration agencies in recent decades, residents of coal mining communities lack a sense of personal or community agency in political and economic spheres and are susceptible to populist politics. Thus, the restoration of a sense of autonomy and voice is a prerequisite for attempts to rebuild mining communities as places contained locally embedded assets that meet human needs.[36]

Fullilove generates the idea of "root shock" to describe the trauma of disruptive socio-economic change, deriving the concept from a study of the African American experience of "urban renewal", which often resulted in the complete erasure of communities. "Root shock" represents "the traumatic stress reaction to the destruction of all or parts of one's emotional ecosystem".[37]

> Root shock undermines trust, increases anxiety, about letting loved ones out of one's sight, destabilises relationships, destroys social, emotional and financial resources, and increases the risk for every kind of stress-related disease, from depression to heart attack.[38]

Fullilove emphasises the critical role of the decline of the built environment, especially its destruction, in causing "root shock". The destruction of familiar buildings and spaces, street scenes and "desire paths" can cause disorientation, especially when it occurs on a large scale, because these structures provide the scaffolding of our life. Human memory is spatial. For these reasons:

> A shared space such as a street can be a locus of collective memory in a double sense. It can express group identity from above, through architectural order, monuments and symbols, commemorative sites, street names, civic spaces, and historic conservation; and it can express the accumulation of memories from below, through the physical and associative traces left by interweaving patterns of everyday life.[39]

Research undertaken for English Heritage, an agency of the UK government concerned with historic monuments, buildings, landscapes and places, suggests that landmark buildings give tangibility to people's sense of civic identity.[40] This is not so much a product of the architectural merit of individual buildings but more a product of the role they play in connecting people with their civic, family and local histories. In addition to churches and banks, department stores held particular meaning. Every-day buildings used by the mass of people held greatest significance, reminding people of their communal past. When well-loved buildings are allowed to fall into disrepair, this can be experienced as a loss of civic pride. Greve et al. provide evidence in the case of Germany that interaction and between economic decline and the loss of significant heritage sites fuels electoral support for populist parties.[41]

The desire to protect familiar streetscapes rests on an instinctive understanding that their regeneration could contribute to broader civic renewal of places. Attributes of the built environment are attached to industrial heritage which contributes to local identity and the stories people tell about the history of their family and place. This is not just perceived by older people but also by younger generations.[42] (Indeed, our own focus groups with school children in Sacriston, discussed in chapter 7, found a perhaps surprising degree of knowledge, interest and attachment to local history.) What Honig calls "public things" offer and embody "stability, adhesion, attachment, resilience, concerns and care" that form the underpinnings local and national identity. Moreover, "They do not take of our *needs* only. They also constitute us, complement us, limit us, thwart us, and interpellate us into democratic citizenship." For Honig, "They are sites of attachment and meanings that occasion the inaugurations, conflicts, contestations that underwrite everyday citizenships and democratic sovereignties."[43]

> "Left-behind" places are not merely aggregations of statistics but are "moral communities", that generate belonging and attachment. In most cases, they have experienced not merely economic decline but the loss of a way of life, a communal bereavement. The destruction of familiar landmarks symbolises this loss, contributes to root shock and forms the background to the formation of political attitudes.

2.4 COMMITMENTS TO PLACE

In the context of urban and regional decline, the question arises: Why do people stay, even if they have the opportunity to leave and what are the consequences of this? In part, high barriers to social and geographical mobility explain strong place attachments.[44] But there is more to the story than this. Wuthnow's account of "left behind" America draws on hundreds of interviews in small communities, paying particular attention to the accounts people give of why they live where they live. In such places, people "recognize the disadvantages of living where they do, and yet they weigh these disadvantages of living where they do against the obligations they feel to their children and, perhaps to aging parents, and to themselves".[45] According to Wuthnow, rural America places particular value on self-reliance whenever possible, but also on the expectation of neighbourly assistance whenever required.[46] In the UK, strong traditions of local collective action marked former coalmining villages (see chapter 4). Strong place attachments have their origins in these traditions, as we show later. For some, at least, such attachments underpin active decisions to stay and contribute, even in the face of population decline, a lack of (good) jobs, brain drain and increasing social problems.

Teti draws on the experience of the Calabrian village where he grew up and which has experienced population loss through emigration, to conclude that staying behind is not an easy decision but an active and difficult process. He uses the term "*restanza*" to describe this choice, which implies a state of staying and resilience.[47] According to Gaudioso:

> *Restanza* means choosing to stay in a place in a conscious active and proactive way by actively guarding it, being aware of the past while enhancing what remains with an impulse towards the future where a new community is possible. In this sense, staying is a dynamic concept, it is a form of journey, a manner to affirm a different existence and existence made of presence and action to hinder absence and abandonment. Presence brings life back, places become liveable and are perceived as sources of opportunities not only for the ones who stay, but also for those who arrive. Moreover, the meaning of staying, is strictly linked with inhabiting as an intense relationship that is characterised by enjoyment and realisation of resources and, at the same time, by care of collective assets.[48]

Píša and Hruška examine the motivations of "agents of change" in Czech old industrial towns and the way these are shaped by local and regional identity. These are people who stay or return to "left behind places" to effects social and economic improvements. Motivations reflect the interplay of local embeddedness of actors, perceptions of local development problems and the identification of "windows of opportunity" for action. What seems crucial is the accumulation of "emotional capital" in particular places, which agents draw upon to frame their action.[49]

In this analysis, "left behind" places are marked by an ethic of care, "a species of activity that includes everything we do to maintain, continue, and repair our world so that we may live in it as well as possible".[50] The (re)builders of social infrastructure are carers for place, stewards of community. Wynn et al., in work in a slate mining community in Blaenau Ffestiniog in Wales, investigate the importance of attachment to place for those who could leave but chose to stay. Drawing on survey data, they identify how stayers describe their choices in terms of a "narrative of attachment", which, in this case, is culturally reinforced by being embedded in a place where Welsh is the lingua franca. Crucially, identities do not concern attempts to maintain existing social and economic structures in aspic but affect a capacity for reinvention while maintaining an attachment to people and place. Wynn et al. ask, "what if we displace the idea of left behind by thinking about staying behind as an active, positive choice not the default of the less capable and adventurous?".[51] This has echoes of Jonathan Lear's suggestion that faced with the end of a way of life, social alternatives arise from acts of "radical hope"—a practical responses to the end of a way of life—that are the product of a sense of belonging and deep attachments that both draw upon and produce commitments to place but are founded on flexibility and openness, and act as a weapon against despair and a means to survive the end of your world. Radical hope is "directed toward a future goodness that transcends the current ability to understand what it is" and "anticipates a good for which those who have hope but as yet lack the appropriate concepts with which to understand it".[52] The effect this leap of faith is to make hope practical rather than despair convincing.[53] This observation seems highly relevant to debates about the remaking of social infrastructure and is borne out by the findings of our study of a Durham mining village.

2.5 BUILDING SOCIAL INFRASTRUCTURE

Social infrastructure may take a range of forms, but its purpose is to provide opportunities for gathering. For Klinenberg, opportunities to gather are critical because this creates spaces for differences to be aired civilly, differences resolved and collective action agreed upon. This echoes Oldenburg's promotion of the idea of "third places" that bring people out of the home and workplace to mix with others, broadening their awareness of local life: "nothing contributes as much to one's sense of belonging to a community as a 'membership' of a third place".[54] For Yarker, social infrastructure creates opportunities for encounter that provide the basis for the accumulation of social capital.[55]

Frankenberg's seminal anthropology of village life in North Wales focused on the activities of a choir, brass band, dramatic society, football club and carnival, which he understands as symbols of the desire for community and means to promote local identity. The village, "Pentrediwaith", presents itself to the outsider as a well-ordered and quiet place, but Frankenberg shows that there are numerous axes of division—e.g., language, religion—that produce conflicts but that these remain hidden "beneath the surface of village life".[56] Outward civility and friendship ensure that conflicts operate within common values and a desire for unity. The chapel, church, football club and parish council provide the local agora in which differences are managed, overlooked or forgiven. In a sense, social infrastructure provides a version of Jane Jacobs' "eyes on the street", which unobtrusively ensure civic order.[57]

Although the purpose of social infrastructure typically is to provide services, sociality is an essential component of how this primary function is enacted.[58] Social infrastructure contributes to capacity-building, facilitates the freedom to gather and provides opportunities for mixing, even if this is not always harmonious or uncontested.[59] The absence of social infrastructure, according to Early Action Taskforce, a national pressure group, results in "civic inequality".[60] While Klinenberg's definition highlights the importance of its built environment component, social infrastructure also comprises less visible, more intangible aspects, that is, "the networks of formal and informal groups, organisations, partnerships, activities and initiatives that both benefit from and sustain the physical and social fabric of a place".[61] Assessing the value of social infrastructure is complicated by the fact that its affordances are several, escaping the calculus of conventional cost–benefit ratios: a public library can simultaneously be a repository of books and a place of learning, a source of commercial support for small businesses and/or somewhere to keep warm or overcome loneliness. Deficiencies in social infrastructure in "left behind" places, then, are a component of urban and regional inequality. Moreover, there is evidence of public demand for improved social infrastructure in "left behind" places. A UK poll suggested that places to meet and other community facilities which bring people together were the ranked first as priority for local action by respondents in "left behind" places.[62]

An explosion of research on social infrastructure either attempts to measure, quantify, index its (non-)provision or sketch cases studies of its operation. Efforts have been made to calculate the return on investment in social infrastructure. Frontier Economics estimated that a £1 million investment in community-led social infrastructure in "left behind" places in the UK could generate approximately £1.2 million of fiscal benefits and £2 million of social and economic benefits over a 10-year period.[63] The Bennett Institute, however, suggests governments are biased towards large-scale physical infrastructure projects aimed at improving connectivity between urban centres and satellite suburbs and towns. But, it suggests:

> micro-level interventions that seek to restore decaying community infrastructure and dilapidated town centres, or that aim to support local initiatives to improve facilities and upgrade amenities, may be far more beneficial in social and economic terms than policymakers have generally appreciated.[64]

In the UK, the "non-statutory" status of libraries, community centres, markets and other components of social infrastructure contributes to their long-term marginalisation within the funding priorities of local authorities, where they have been particularly vulnerable to successive budget cuts over a decade of austerity after 2010, particularly affecting "left behind" places.

Beyond a narrow economic calculus, social infrastructure can contribute to broader human well-being. In the field of disaster management, strong infrastructure is seen as allowing societies to overcome collective action problems, accumulate civic capital and offer better guarantees of the provision of mutual aid and informal insurance during shocks when standard providers of assistance may be out of service or unable to assist.[65] According to Haldane, the COVID-19 pandemic demonstrated the value of social infrastructure in supporting "the left-behind and left-alone".[66] Communities rallied to strengthen existing networks and create new mutual aid groups, replenishing social capital as other forms of capital depreciated, evidenced by increased numbers of people began volunteering. Klinenberg acknowledges the importance of volunteering but points to the importance of social infrastructure as providing the space in which this can occur. For many, volunteering is as much about being with other people and the emotional benefits this brings as it about completing a project.[67]

Sir Michael Marmot argues that improvements in social infrastructure are crucial to improving health outcomes in "left behind" places.[68] Social and clinical conditions are linked and shaped by the presence or absence of social infrastructure. For instance, recent analysis shows rising levels of loneliness in Europe, albeit this is geographically uneven.[69] Klinenberg suggests that there are more people living alone that any time in history, raising the risk of loneliness among those prone to isolation, such as the elderly. The US Surgeon General has identified an epidemic of loneliness, which has negative health impacts.[70] Loneliness increases the risk of emotional disorders such as depression, anxiety and substance abuse, but also puts people at greater risk of physical ailments that seem unrelated, such as heart disease, cancer, stroke, hypertension, dementia and premature death.[71] In England, levels of loneliness seem higher in "left behind" places and worsened during the COVID-19 pandemic.[72] This recent concern echoes earlier work about the human costs of isolation.[73] Infrastructures that help people to overcome loneliness have potentially far-reaching impacts on health, which in turn may have positive economic impacts.

Andy Haldane, former Chief Economist of the Bank England, argues that the absence of social infrastructure hinders economic development, particularly through the depletion of social capital. When social infrastructure is lost, social capital depreciates "and [offers] another reason to feel left-behind".[74] Concerns about the loss of social infrastructure are widespread. Oldenburg sees the third spaces being undermined by car-born, privatised forms of suburban living in the US. He romanticises the English pub or the French café as alternatives, but these institutions are in crisis, especially in "left behind" places. Quershi and Fyans identify the English pub as a form of social infrastructure and contributor to a sense of community cohesion, albeit one under threat.[75] A visit to the local pub serves as an occasion to leave one's house and socialise with neighbours and friends, helping prevent social isolation and loneliness, especially in small towns and villages where the range of social infrastructure is narrower than found in cities. But 7000 pubs closed in England and Wales between 2012 and 2021,[76] and closures occurred disproportionately in "left behind" places. Bolet, examining the period 2013–16, finds that people in areas that experienced pub closures were more than 4 percentage points more likely to vote for the populist United Kingdom Independence Party (UKIP), supporting the argument that the loss of social infrastructure fuels a sense of local decline, isolation and "left behindness" that foments the appeal of populist politics.[77] Within the "*La France périphérique*", the loss of village cafés and bistros symbolises the creation of the left behind France.[78] Action to arrest the decline of social infrastructure was a theme in Marine Le Pen's political campaign to win the support of "Forgotten France" in the 2022 Presidential Election.[79] Within the Netherlands, a growing political gap between the Randstad conurbation and provinces such as Drenthe, Friesland, Limburg, Zeeland and Groningen, brought to international attention in 2022 via farmer protests against the Dutch government's environmental reforms, also expresses a broader anger about the loss of social infrastructure.[80] Research by the Pew Research Center, based on focus groups in the US and UK, noted that a sense of being "left behind" was informed by experiences of industrial restricting and the decline of high streets, but also by the closure of local pubs and clubs:

> These places were viewed as key community-building institutions, and their loss was seen as a death knell of social cohesion in their area, ushered in by changing business and industry. Groups described local pubs as gathering spaces for members of the community to build relationships and get to know each other, discussing how their closure meant people did not bond anymore. Youth clubs were also seen as pillars of communities, and groups suggested that their demise has pushed young people onto the streets to cause mischief and engage in criminal activity.[81]

2.6 CONCLUSIONS

Given the long history of poor outcomes from policies designed to improve conditions in "left behind" places, there is widening acceptance of the need to better understand the multiple and connected dimensions of geographical disadvantage that include economic, social, environmental, health, infrastructural, cultural and political factors and the multifaceted nature of "left behind" places. Moreover, places are not just aggregates of economic indicators but a focus for identities, belonging and attachments. Given the failure of conventional forms of economic development in "left behind" places, MacKinnon et al. point to the value of approaches that are founded on peoples' visions and potentials rather externally determined programmes.[82] Neo-endogenous approaches address problems of low service provision, ageing populations, isolation and lack of critical mass for economic development, which mark many "left behind" places. As we show below, such approaches also address the complex relationship between the effective and material dimension of left behindness, because they draw upon communal resources. As we show in chapter 7, the remaking of social infrastructure in Sacriston is focused on addressing unmet needs. Social infrastructure provides an ingredient in the new recipes for local development, but one that, in crucial respects, mirrors earlier efforts described in chapter 5.

The above discussion has demonstrated growing policy interest in social infrastructure in "left behind" places in the UK (and elsewhere). In the UK and elsewhere the debate has been dominated by studies undertaken by several think tanks and commissions, many of which are cited in this review of the literature. Outputs fall into two main types. First, there are efforts to measure, quantify and index places in terms of the (non-)provision of social infrastructure and its consequences. Second, several reports provide pen portraits of examples of social infrastructure provision. While valuable, such contributions tend to offer rather static and aggregate accounts of the provision of social infrastructure, leaving a gap for deeper, more historical and qualitative understandings of the conditions under which it is made, unmade and remade. Specifically, our empirical work, from the beginning, highlighted the importance of local attachments in explaining the making, unmaking and remaking of social infrastructure, but this has received scant attention in the existing literature. Therefore, we propose a deeper engagement with the making, unmaking and remaking of social infrastructure. We identify the (re)builders of social infrastructure as carers for place, stewards of community. This has implications for policy that are developed later. In the following chapter we set out some methods to achieve a deeper understanding of place and inform our policy implications.

NOTES

1. Pike A, Rodriguez-Pose A and Tomaney J (2017) *Local and Regional Development*, 2nd ed. London: Routledge. https://doi.org/10.4324/9781315767673
2. Martin R, Gardiner B, Pike A, Sunley P and Tyler P (2022) *Levelling Up Left Behind Places. The Scale and Nature of the Economic and Policy Challenge*. London: Taylor & Francis. https://doi.org/10.4324/9781032244341
3. Velthuis S, MacKinnon D, Pike A and Tomaney J (2023) Types of "left-behind places" in the EU15. *Town and Country Planning*, 92(1): 28–31.
4. Pike A, Béal V, Cauchi-Duval N, Frankl R, Kinossian N, Lang T, Leibert T, MacKinnon D, Rousseau M, Royer J, Servillo L, Tomaney J and Velthuis S (2023) "Left behind places": A geographical etymology. *Regional Studies*. https://doi.org/10.1080/00343404.2023.2167972
5. Klinenberg E (2020) *Palaces for People. How to Build a More Equal and United Society*. London: Vintage, at 151.
6. All Party Parliamentary Group on Left Behind Neighbourhoods (2020) *Communities of Trust: Why We Must Invest in Social Infrastructure of "Left Behind" Neighbourhoods*. https://www.appg-leftbehind-neighbourhoods.org.uk/wp-content/uploads/2021/03/8118-APPG-Communities-Report-NEW.pdf
7. Local Trust (2019) *Left Behind? Understanding Communities on the Edge*. London: Local Trust. https://localtrust.org.uk/insights/research/left-behind-understanding-communities-on-the-edge/
8. Pike et al. (2023), see Reference 4.
9. Rodríguez-Pose A (2018) The revenge of the places that don't matter (and what to do about it). *Cambridge Journal of Regions, Economy and Society*, 11(1): 189–209. https://doi.org/10.1093/cjres/rsx024
10. Institute of Fiscal Studies (IFS) (2020) Levelling up: Where and how? In *IFS Green Budget 2020*. https://ifs.org.uk/publications/15055.
11. For an attempt to index left behindness along different dimensions, see Furlong J (2019) The changing electoral geography of England and Wales: Varieties of "left-behindedness". *Political Geography*, 75. https://doi.org/10.1016/j.polgeo.2019.102061
12. Mackinnon D, Kempton L, O'Brien P, Ormerod E, Pike A and Tomaney J (2022) Reframing urban and regional "development" for "left behind" places. *Cambridge Journal of Regions, Economy and Society*, 15(1): 39–56. https://doi.org/10.1093/cjres/rsab034
13. For instance, Glaeser E (2011) *Triumph of the City*. London: Pan.

14 Seamus Heaney, quoted in O'Toole F (2023) Seamus Heaney: His death 10 years ago was "the end of a great eloquence". *Irish Times*, 26 August. https://www.irishtimes.com/culture/books/2023/08/26/the-end-of-a-great-eloquence-remembering-seamus-heaney-10-years-on-by-fintan-otoole/

15 Wuthnow R (2019) *The Left Behind: Decline and Rage in Small-Town America*. Princeton, NJ: Princeton University Press, at 18.

16 Bellah R, Madsen R, Sullivan W, Swindler A and Tipton S (1985) *Habits of the Heart. Individualism and Commitment in American Life*. Berkeley, CA: University of California Press, at 153.

17 Wuthnow (2019), at 96, see Reference 15.

18 For a review of the positive psychological impacts of nostalgia, see Sedikides C, Wildshut T, Arndt J and Routledge C (2008) Nostalgia: Past present and future. *Current Directions in Psychological Science*, 17(5): 304–307. https://doi.org/10.1111/j.1467-8721.2008.00595.x

19 Teti V (2018) *Stones into Bread*, trans. F Lorrigio and D Pietropaolo. Toronto, ON: Guernica, at 11.

20 Bellah et al. (1985), at 152, see Reference 16.

21 Teti (2018), at 192, see Reference 19.

22 Olick J K, Vinitzky-Seroussi V and Levy D (2011) Introduction. In O J Vinitzky-Seroussi and D Levy (eds.), *The Collective Memory Reader*, pp. 3–61. Oxford: Oxford University Press.

23 Hwalbachs M (1992). *On Collective Memory*, trans L Coser. Chicago, IL: Chicago University Press.

24 Prendergast J (2021) *Attachment economics: Everyday pioneers for the next economy*. https://medium.com/onioncollective/attachment-economics-everyday-pioneers-for-the-next-economy-d0a9ac20080

25 Weil S (1952) *The Need for Roots*. London: Routledge.

26 See especially Devine-Wright P and Howes Y (2010) Disruption to place attachment and the protection of restorative environments: A wind energy case study. *Journal of Environmental Psychology*, 30(3): 271–280. https://doi.org/10.1016/j.jenvp.2010.01.008. More broadly, see Manzo L and Devine-Wright P (eds.) (2014) *Place Attachment*. London: Routledge.

27 The classic statement of attachment in theory in the psychological literature is Bowlby J (1982) *Attachment and Loss*. New York: Basic; see also Kraemer S and Roberts J (1996) *The Politics of Attachment*. London: Free Association Book.

28 Manzo L and Perkins D (2006) Finding common ground: The importance of place attachment to community participation and planning. *Journal of Planning Literature*, 20(4): 335–350, at 347. https://doi.org/10.1177/0885412205286160

29 Marris P (1986) *Loss and Change*, 2nd ed. London: Routledge & Kegan Paul; Marris P (1996) *The Politics of Uncertainty. Attachment in Private and Public Life*. London Routledge.

30 Mattinson D (2020) *Beyond the Red Wall: Why Labour Lost, How the Conservatives Won and What Will Happen Next?* London: Biteback.

31 Görmar F (2023) Loss and change: Culture narratives in old industrial regions in East Germany. *Regional Science Policy and Practice*. https://doi.org/10.1111/rsp3.12689

32 Silver L, Schumacher S, Mordecai M, Greenwood S and Keegan M (2020) *In U.S. and UK, Globalisation Leaves Some Feeling "Left Behind" or "Swept Up"* (October). Pew Research Center. https://www.pewresearch.org/global/2020/10/05/in-u-s-and-uk-globalization-leaves-some-feeling-left-behind-or-swept-up/

33 Wuthnow (2019), at 56, see Reference 15.

34 Prendergast (2021), see Reference 24.

35 Wuthnow (2019), at 78, see Reference 15.

36 Abreu M and Jones C (2021) The shadow of the pithead: Understanding social and political attitudes in former coal mining communities in the UK. *Applied Geography*, 131. https://doi.org/10.1016/j.apgeog.2021.102448

37 Fullilove M (2016) *Root Shock. How Tearing Up City Neighborhoods Hurts America, and What We Can Do About It.* New York: NYU Press, at 11.

38 Fullilove (2016), at 14, see Reference 37.

39 Hebbert M (2005). The street as a locus of collective memory. *Environment and Planning D: Society and Space*, 23: 592. https://doi.org/10.1068/d55j

40 Public First (2022) *Heritage and Civic Pride. Report for Historic England.* https://www.publicfirst.co.uk/heritage-and-civic-pride-public-first-report-for-historic-england.html

41 Greve M, Fritsch M and Wyrwich M (2023) Long-term decline of regions and the rise of populism: The case of Germany. *Journal of Regional Science*, 63(2): 409–405. https://doi.org/10.1111/jors.12627

42 Grimshaw L and Mates L (2021) "It's part of our community, where we lives": Urban heritage ands children's sense of place. *Urban Studies*, 59(7): 1334–1352. https://doi.org/10.1177/00420980211019597

43 Honig B (2017) *Public Things. Democracy in Disrepair.* New York, NY: Fordham University Press, pp. 4–6. https://doi.org/10.2307/j.ctt1xhr6n9

44 Hann B (2021) Voyages around father. Class, community and mobility in industrial South Wales. In Morgan W J and Bowie F (eds.), *Social Anthropologies of the Welsh*, pp. 241–259. Hereford: Sean Kingston.

45 Wuthnow (2018), see Reference 15.

46 On this point, see also Bellah et al. (1985), at 153, see Reference 16.

47 Teti (2018), see Reference 19.

48 Gaudioso D (2021) *Shrinking Areas as Dynamic Spaces of Care and Resilience.* https://www.welcomingspaces.eu/tag/restanza/. For an application of these ideas in the context of Welsh rural community, see Wynn L C, Froud J and Williams K (2020) *A Way Ahead? Empowering Restanza in a Slate Valley.* https://foundationaleconomycom.files.wordpress.com/2022/04/restanza-english-version-as-of-7-feb-2022.pdf

49 Píša J and Hruška V (2023) "It was my duty to change this place": Motivations of agents of change in Czech old industrial towns. *Geografiska Annaler: Series B, Human Geography.* https://doi.org/10.1080/04353684.2023.2208580

50 Tronto J C (2015). *Who Cares? How to Reshape a Democratic Politics.* Ithaca, NY: Cornell University Press. https://www.jstor.org/stable/10.7591/j.ctt18kr598

51 Tronto (2015), at 4, see Reference 50.

52 Lear J (2008) *Radical Hope. Ethics in the Face of Cultural Devastation*. Cambridge, MA: Harvard University Press, at 103. https://www.jstor.org/stable/j.ctvjz82p7

53 Williams R (1989) *Resources of Hope. Culture, Democracy, Socialism*. London: Verso.

54 Oldenburg R (1989) *The Great Good Place*. New York, NY: Paragon House, at xxiii.

55 Yarker S (2022) *Creating Spaces for an Ageing Society: The Role of Critical Social Infrastructure*. Bingley: Emerald.

56 Frankenberg R (1957) *Village on the Border. A Social Study of Religion, Politics and Football in a North Wales Community*. London: Cohen & West, at 17.

57 Jacobs J (1961) *Death and Life of Great American Cities*. New York, NY: Vintage, at 32.

58 Latham A and Layton J (2019) Social infrastructure and the public life of cities: Studying urban sociality and public spaces. *Geography Compass*. https://doi.org/10.1111/gec3.12444

59 Layton J and Latham A (2021) Social infrastructure and public life—Notes on Finsbury Park, London. *Urban Geography*, 43(5): 755–756 https://doi.org/10.1080/02723638.2021.1934631

60 Early Action Task Force (2020) *Being in a Good Place. Investing in Social Infrastructure*, at 4. http://www.civilexchange.org.uk/wp-content/uploads/2020/12/Good-Place-Report-Final.pdf

61 All Party Parliamentary Group on Left Behind Neighbourhoods (2020) *Communities of Trust: Why We Must Invest in the Social Infrastructure of "Left Behind" Neighbourhoods*. https://www.appg-leftbehindneighbourhoods.org.uk/publication/communities-of-trust-why-we-must-invest-in-the-infrastructure-of-left-behind-neighbourhoods/; Power to Change (2021) *Building Our Social Infrastructure: Why Levelling Up Means Creating a More Socially Connected Britain*. London: Power to Change. https://www.powertochange.org.uk/wp-content/uploads/2021/10/XX-Building-our-social-infrastructure-FINAL.pdf; Slocock C (2018) *Valuing Social Infrastructure*. London: Civil Exchange. http://www.civilexchange.org.uk/wp-content/uploads/2018/06/Valuing-Social-Infrastructure-final.pdf

62 Survation (2020) *"Red Wall" Voters like Where They Live, Want More Places to Meet and Support for the Young*. https://www.survation.com/red-wall-voters-like-where-they-live-want-more-places-to-meet-and-support-for-the-young/

63 Frontier Economics (2021) *The Impacts of Social Infrastructure Investment*. https://localtrust.org.uk/wp-content/uploads/2021/07/Frontier-Economics_the-impacts-of-social-infrastructure-investment.pdf

64 Bennett Institute for Public Policy (2021) *Townscapes. The Value of Social Infrastructure*. Cambridge: Bennett Institute, at 57. https://www.bennettinstitute.cam.ac.uk/publications/social-infrastructure/; see also Early Action Task Force (2020), see Reference 60.

65 Aldrich P (2021) The benefits of social infrastructure and civic ties in uncertain times. *East Asia Forum Quarterly*, July–September: 26–27.

66 Haldane A (2020) Reweaving the social fabric after the crisis. *Financial Times*, 24 April. https://www.ft.com/content/fbb1ef1c-7ff8-11ea-b0fb-13524ae1056b

67 Wuthnow (2019), see Reference 45.

68 Institute of Health Equity (2020) *Health Equity in England: The Marmot Review 10 Years On.* https://www.instituteofhealthequity.org/resources-reports/marmot-review-10-years-on/the-marmot-review-10-years-on-full-report.pdf

69 Burlina C and Rodríguez-Pose A (2022) *Alone and Lonely. The Economic Cost of Solitude for Regions in Europe* (Papers in Evolutionary Economic Geography No. 21/33). Department of Human Geography and Planning, Utrecht University. http://econ.geo.uu.nl/peeg/peeg2133.pdf

70 US Surgeon General (2023) *Our Epidemic of Loneliness and Isolation. The U.S. Surgeon General's Advisory on the Healing Effects of Social Connection and Community.* https://www.hhs.gov/sites/default/files/surgeon-general-social-connection-advisory.pdf

71 For reviews of the clinical evidence, see Heinrich L and Gullone E (2006) The clinical significance of loneliness: A literature review. *Clinical Psychology Review*, 26(6): 695–718. https://doi.org/10.1016/j.cpr.2006.04.002; Holt-Lunstad J, Robles T F, Sbarra D A (2017) Advancing social connection as a public health priority in the United States. *American Psychologist*, 72(6): 517–530. https://psycnet.apa.org/doi/10.1037/amp0000103; Holt-Lunstad J (2022) Social connection as a public health issue: The evidence and a systemic framework for prioritising the "social" in social determinants of health. *Annual Review of Public Health*, 43(1): 193–213. https://doi.org/10.1146/annurev-publhealth-052020-110732

72 Office for National Statistics (ONS) (2021) *Mapping Loneliness During the Coronavirus Pandemic.* Exeter: ONS. https://www.ons.gov.uk/peoplepopulationandcommunity/wellbeing/articles/mappinglonelinessduringthecoronaviruspandemic/2021-04-07_

73 Putnam R (2000) *Bowling Alone: The Collapse and Revival of American Community.* New York, NY: Simon & Shuster.

74 Haldane A (2019) Ashington—Speech given at St. James' Park, Newcastle upon Tyne. 24 September, at 6. https://industrialstrategycouncil.org/sites/default/files/2019-09/Ashington%20-%20Andrew%20G%20Haldane%20speech%20(24%20September%202019).pdf

75 Qureshi Z and Fyans J (2021) *The Power of Pubs. Protecting Social Infrastructure and Laying the Groundwork for Levelling Up.* London: Localis. https://localis.org.uk/research/the-power-of-pubs/

76 BBC News (2022) *Pub Numbers Fall to Lowest on Record.* https://www.bbc.co.uk/news/business-62031833

77 Bolet D (2021) Drinking alone: Local socio-cultural degradation and radical right support—The case of British pub closures. *Comparative Political Studies*, 54(9): 1653–1692. https://doi.org/10.1177/0010414021997158

78 Gulluy C (2015) *La France périphérique: Comment on a sacrifié les classes populaires.* Paris: Flammarion.

79 Abboud L and Nolsoe E (2022) The corner of France that explains Macron, Le Pen and a deep political divide. *Financial Times*, 14 April. https://www.ft.com/content/5bd5e791-9561-42a0-ac8c-f5bdeeb81309

80 Adriaanse M (2020) Revanche van de "plekken die er niet meer toe doen". *NRC Handelsblad*, 29 July. https://www.nrc.nl/nieuws/2022/07/29/revanche-van-de-plekken-die-er-niet-meer-toe-doen-a4137759

81 Silver et al. (2020), see Reference 32.

82 We draw here on Mackinnon et al. (2022), see Reference 12.

3. Methods: researching the affective dimensions of "left behind places" to underpin new policy approaches

Keywords: pragmatist inquiry; mixed methods; critical cases; deep place study

3.1 THE METHODOLOGICAL CHALLENGE

We noted in chapter 2 the several attempts to quantify, index and tabulate the provision of social infrastructure in "left behind places". One important contribution from the OCSI/Local Trust identifies the provision of social infrastructure focusing on three domains: "civic assets" (including pubs, libraries, green space, community centres, swimming pools, etc.); "connectedness" (e.g., access to key services, such as health services, within a reasonable travel distance, available public transport and digital infrastructure); and "community engagement" (e.g., local charities, participation in civic life, etc.). Indicators—in the form of publicly available secondary data—are gathered for the three domains and an index is created to map social infrastructure provision. The OCSI/Local Trust suggests that "civic assets, community engagement and connectivity, make a significant difference to social and economic outcomes for people and communities".[1] We use the OCSI/Local Trust's Community Needs Index to identify County Durham as a suitable subject for our research (see below).

While it useful to know about the distribution of social infrastructure, this still leaves a gap in our understanding of the processes by which social infrastructure is made, unmade and remade. The process of identifying "left behind places" relies principally on static indicators that represent a specific moment in time and thus fail to reveal the reasons a place became "left behind" and in what way.[2] Much existing work on social infrastructure in left behind places similarly presents a static picture of social infrastructure provision offering few insights into how these patterns are produced. Moreover, in chapter 2, we noted the complexity of social infrastructure, comprising a mix of the hard and soft, formal and informal, tangible and intangible. A partial, historical understanding may lead us to draw erroneous conclusions about the making, unmaking and remaking of social infrastructure. For instance, the OCSI/Local Trust asserts that the deterioration of social infrastructure "is doubtless related to austerity and the cuts in public services and welfare benefits it ushered in".[3] Our research challenges this assertion, emphasising much longer term processes operating alongside more recent events and complex relationships between soft and hard, tangible and intangible infrastructures. While not denying the importance of austerity, our methods allow us to show that the making, unmaking and remaking of social infrastructure occurred over a century or more, of which post-2010 austerity is only an episode. Attributing the loss of social infrastructure to recent austerity could lead to faulty policy recommendations, focusing on short-term measures rather the longer term ones necessary to build resilient social infrastructure.

To augment the emergent body of quantitative research, we have developed a set of mixed methods suited to developing a historical and geographical perspective on the making, unmaking and remaking of social infrastructure. Sayer's distinction between extensive and intensive methods is a useful first step for thinking about the value of mixed methods and their appropriateness for the study we report here.[4] In this account, extensive methods are descriptive and helpful for identifying patterns, but have limited explanatory power. Intensive

https://doi.org/10.1080/2578711X.2023.2254998

research focuses primarily on causal structures and secondarily on the contingent conditions operating in particular instances. Knowledge here is gained through more qualitative methods and has a crucial contextualising dimension situating data in time and space. As Sayer notes, these two groups of methods are complementary. Indeed, we draw on data produced via extensive methods to inform the directions of intensive research in Sacriston in County Durham. Moreover, intensive forms of research—including the mixed methods we use here—in turn, can be used to develop hypotheses for further quantitative or comparative work. Adapting a term from remote sensing, our aim here is to "ground truth"[5] general claims about social infrastructure in left behind places that are inferred from statistical analysis by developing an account based on direct observation of the phenomenon in question. We achieve this objective through a deep-place case study of the making, unmaking and remaking of social infrastructure in one village, providing a richer and more contextualised account than hitherto available and to offer insights to policymakers. Moreover, as noted in chapter 2, "left behindness" is multidimensional, comprising material and affective dimensions. It speaks not only of material conditions that are measured comparatively easily but also of perceptions and intersubjective understandings, which our methods enable us to grasp.[6]

3.2 A PRAGMATIST ORIENTATION TO INQUIRY

Our epistemological approach is informed by philosophical pragmatism. We begin by acknowledging academic researchers are at a disadvantage in understanding "left behind places". As a rule, they do not live in, work in or regularly interact with such places. The procedures and rituals of academic life present barriers to communication with those who live and work in such places. As the founder of philosophical pragmatism, Dewey himself noted:

> It is impossible for the high-brows to secure a monopoly of such knowledge as must be used for the regulation of common affairs. In the degree to which they become a specialized class, they are shut off from knowledge of the needs which they are supposed to serve.[7]

Eschewing a "spectator theory of knowledge", "quest for certainty" and firm ideological starting points, Dewey advocates an approach to inquiry that focuses on problems of everyday life to create useful knowledge. The task of researchers is to understand particular concerns, work with communities to facilitate inquiry, collectively develop ideas and practices to produce desired change—to form a "community of inquirers". In modern parlance, this suggests the need for "co-production" of research findings. Moreover, pragmatism, according to Brandom, implies a concern with the production of "intelligent doings rather than abstract sayings".[8]

Pragmatism suggests a "orientation to inquiry" that is open and driven by the concerns of communities—at variegated and indeterminate scales—in order to understand the geo-historical context of actors, institutions and cultures, appreciate the local character of public debate, and listen to conversations that are already underway.[9] It requires an appreciation of diverse truths that exist in the community in relation to the range of issues discussed. The task of researchers, if invited, through conversations or relationships, is to explore the possibility of working on an issue identified as a matter of concern by the participants in the inquiry. Once an issue is identified in this way, engage in some sort of inquiry through methods appropriate to the case. But it is an approach that requires continued dialogue with the community and its interests by maintaining a presence.[10]

In this vein, our focus on the role of social infrastructure arose from initial open-ended conversations with people in Sacriston, as we explored the nature "left behindness". The importance of the making, unmaking and remaking of social infrastructure arose from these discussions. In this sense, we joined conversations already underway and helped form a "community of inquirers". In this study, therefore, we did not test a theory of social infrastructure, but developed one inductively from our observations. There is now an ongoing relationship between the research team and the (re)makers of social infrastructure in Sacriston.[11]

3.3 RESEARCHING SOCIAL INFRASTRUCTURE

Having established our epistemological framework, we deploy a range of methods appropriate to our case. Star notes that infrastructure has several characteristics that lend themselves to research using an ethnographic approach.[12] Among other things, infrastructure is embedded in broader social arrangements and human entanglements and, typically, is a longstanding feature of the built environment. Provisioning of infrastructure extends beyond a single event and is shaped by the conventions of a community of practice. It builds on installed bases and does not grow *de novo*, becomes visible upon breakdown and is fixed in modular increments not in a single episode. Ethnography offers the opportunity to "ground" theory—in this case of social infrastructure—in lived practices and experiences. Attention to the lived experience of people in "left behind places", their practices, perspectives and aspirations, "produces an analysis that challenges the dominant instrumental view of urban planning".[13] Mattila et al. make a strong case for using ethnographic methods in urban and regional planning as a means of breaching the gap between communicative methods that seek to elicit inter-subjective consensus (participatory planning) and "knowledge-based" approaches (oriented toward quantitative analysis and the production of abstract or generic place-based data).[14] Ethnographic approaches promise a means to identify the temporalities and geographies of social infrastructure, the contribution of local actors to its production, the nature of any conflicts and the gendered character of access to it.[15]

These observations seem especially pertinent in the case of social infrastructure. Frankenberg's classic study in the 1950s of the village of "Pentrediwaith" (see chapter 2) shows that activities that begin for the purposes of recreation—a choir, brass band, dramatic society, football club, carnival—offer a means to promote local identity.[16] These activities are contested and involve both the creation and the abandonment of activities—the making, unmaking and remaking of social infrastructure. Frankenberg's year-long engagement with the village allowed him to identify "a series of activities which, though started for recreation, symbolized their desire to be a community".[17] Life in "Pentrediwaith" was bedevilled by conflicts, which were rarely directly expressed and operated below outward shows of civility and friendship and within an overall acceptance of common values and goals.

As a foundational text in the "Manchester School of Anthropology", Frankenberg's study pioneered the "extended case method", which focuses on the detailed study of concrete empirical cases with a view to "extract" general principles from specific observations. Burawoy proposes:

> The extended case method applies reflexive science to ethnography in order to extract the general from the unique, to move from the "micro" to the "macro", and to connect the present to the past in anticipation of the future, all by building pre-existing theory.[18]

The extended case method allows us to move between analytical levels, allowing attention to the micro-, meso- and macro-scales and their interrelationships. To achieve this, fieldwork combines historical and documentary analysis, interviews and observations to elucidate social processes in bounded communities, albeit in a global context, providing insights into the lived experience of social change. We use this framework to inform our choice of appropriate mixed methods and advance the theory of social infrastructure drawing on concepts of place attachment, "root shock" and "radical hope".

We use a case study approach in order to clarify the deeper causes behind the making, unmaking and remaking of social infrastructure rather than to identify the symptoms of the problem or how frequently they occur. Using Flyvbjerg's typology, Sacriston offers us a "critical case"[19] for exploring the provision of social infrastructure in "left behind places" because it exhibits the attributes of the general problem. Klinenberg asserts that "left behind places" were once rich in social infrastructure, but much of this has been lost. Our methods allow us to test this assertion. As Flyvbjerg notes, there are no universal methodological principles to guide the selection of critical cases; instead it relies on experience and judgement to select "most likely" or "least likely" cases. Sacriston presents a "most likely" case because it has a history of social infrastructure-making, has experienced its unmaking, but also offers a contemporary story of resilience and the remaking of social infrastructure.

Informed by an "ethnographic sensibility"..,[20] we deploy a set of mixed methods to investigate our site, the former coal mining village of Sacriston, produced by a "community of inquirers".

To this end, we conducted the study with the Durham Miners' Association, employing an embedded researcher.[21] Wills observes, "All knowledge is co-produced through thinking and acting with others, even is such engagement is often ignored."[22] At issue here is a concern with how research can benefit "left behind places" rather than extract "findings" for academic purposes. Our aim is to undertake research that legitimises and circulates stories that strengthen communities and assists the development of their well-being and contribute to building bottom-up coalitions and networks for development. To this end, we want our research to help build local power and capacity. This requires building collective knowledge and action through long-term engagement and collaboration, founded on relationship-building, listening, collaborating and acting conjointly. Theory-building is displaced in favour of valuing the processes, practice and outcomes of research.

County Durham offers an appropriate site in which to study social infrastructure in "left behind places". It contains a comparatively high proportion of "left behind places", as measured by the UK government's Index of Multiple Deprivation, and is deficient in social infrastructure, according to the analysis undertaken by the OCSI/Local Trust (Figure 3.1). The findings reported here form part of an ongoing study based on relationships with local actors, many of whom are involved in the production and maintenance of the social infrastructure we describe. We see a historical perspective as crucial because, according to Klinenberg, our knowledge of the long-term processes of infrastructure-building and destruction, and its consequences, is limited.[23] Indeed, our analysis reveals that Sacriston was once richly endowed with social infrastructure, but much of this has been lost, yet the processes that produced this outcome are complex and poorly understood. But we also reveal efforts to remake social infrastructure. To this end, we integrate a range of data, including archival and oral history, focus groups with government and other agencies, community organisations and school children, interviews with actors in the village, and cartographic representations in order to capture the lived experience of the community and its relationship to social infrastructure.

The mixed methods approach is a strategy for overcoming each method's weaknesses and limitations by deliberately combining different techniques within the same investigations. For the most part, we standard research methods. What is new here, however, is the planned, systematic synthesis of these different research styles, purposefully aimed at improving social science knowledge.[24] All methods have strengths and weaknesses and integrating the findings from a mixed methods approach to research is always a challenge.[25] The specific methods we deploy are cartography, archival and oral history, site observation, semi-structured interviews with key actors involved in the building and maintenance of social infrastructure and focus groups of providers and users. Each method is tried and tested and each has strengths and weaknesses which are discussed below, but in combination they offer a highly textured, historically informed account of the making, remaking and social infrastructure. We integrate our findings in the form of a narrative of change, intended to convey the scale and complexity of the making, unmaking and remaking social infrastructure.

Figure 3.1. Community Needs Index: community needs score (higher = greater need).

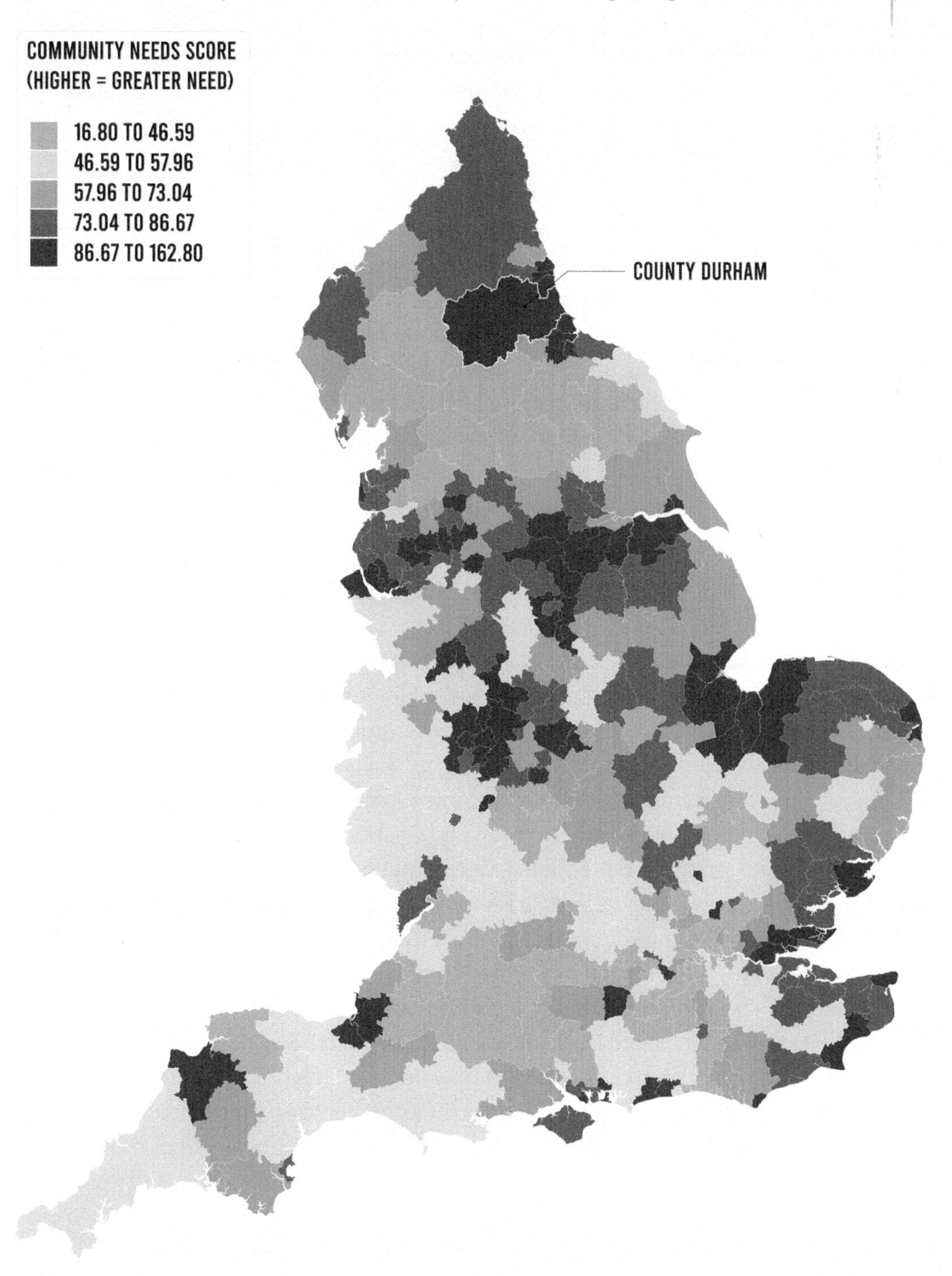

Sources: OCSI/Local Trust, *Local Insight*. https://ocsi.uk/2019/10/21/community-needs-index-measuring-social-and-cultural-factors/; adapted by the authors.
Note: All areas are shown at the local authority level, with County Durham highlighted.

3.4 OUR APPROACH

The research reported here has taken place over several years (and is ongoing), emphasising our concern to develop a long-term and embedded understanding of change, rather than delivering snapshots of events. In addition to employing well-tested social science methods, we have found that regularly spending time in the village—including calling on our informants for a cup of tea, attending local festivals (such as the one that celebrated the Platinum Jubilee of Queen Elizabeth II in 2022 or the annual Durham Miners' Gala), attending church services, taking our students on field visits, or serving as trustees of the organisations we are studying—affords perspectives and insights that arise in unplanned moments which enrich our understanding of village dynamics and inform our understanding of the making, unmaking and remaking of social infrastructure. Such interactions amount to "facework commitments"—that is, the "trust relations which are sustained or expressed in social connections established in circumstances of copresence"[26]—that encourage informants to share information that they might be reluctant to do in more formal settings. Site observations both generate information and influence our interpretation of the data we gather using more formal methods.

We use cartography to reveal the changing historical provision of social infrastructure. Through the analysis of historical maps, the transformation of Sacriston from a paragon of industrial productivity to a "left behind place" is tracked through time, clearly highlighting its rapid growth and slower decline. It starts from a mapping of the basic urban elements and is completed by overlaying the perceptions and additional information that emerged from the broader spectrum of studied data. Using figure ground theory,[27] a hierarchy of urban space and scales was constructed distinguishing the "building blocs" of the territory (i.e., built masses, infrastructure, natural environment) to investigate to what extent the transformation of the physical environment of both Sacriston and County Durham affects the perception of being "left behind". This two-dimensional representation of space was then enriched with publicly available quantitative datasets, a review of the grey literature (such as local government reports) and testimonies from local people to identify the social infrastructure in the village and the way it has changed over time. From this process two key maps were created highlighting the social infrastructure that existed in the town in 1910, around the time of peak coal production in County Durham, and in 2022. This shows how well endowed with social infrastructure Sacriston once was, and how depleted it is now. The use of maps lends itself to pragmatist inquiry, according to Barnes.[28] Cartographical representation promises an experiment in think and the creation of spatial and historical vocabulary to discuss the making, unmaking and remaking of social infrastructure. We presented our maps to residents of Sacriston at a meeting of the Durham County Local History Society in October 2022 in order to test our representation and amended them in light of discussion.

For such a small place, we were able to find a rich record of the historical development of social infrastructure in Sacriston from the late 19th century. The archival sources included local newspapers, the meticulous accounts of local organisations such as the Annfield Plain Industrial Co-operative Society,[29] the Catholic Church,[30] Women's Sections[31] and the Durham Aged Mineworkers' Homes Association,[32] histories of local cricket leagues[33] and biographies of local politicians, such as Peter Lee.[34] Sacriston Working Men's' Club commissioned its own centenary history in 2002.[35] The early builders of social infrastructure took care to record their activities in ways that are very helpful for contemporary researchers and allow us to present a detailed account of its making which throws up lessons for contemporary debates, to which we return in chapter 7.

Oral history is a useful complement to archival research in mapping social infrastructure in the past. While research with archival sources such as maps, newspapers and directories can establish what social infrastructure existed in the past, when it was created and (where appropriate) when it disappeared, this information tells us less about who used this social infrastructure, how and what it meant to local people. Oral history, particularly since the 1980s, has focused on the recovery not only of facts about the pasts but also of the subjective experience of interviewees. It is, of course, the case that interviewees, remembering their town or village 30, 40, 50 or more years ago, sometimes make mistakes in their recollections. But oral history theory suggests that these can, in fact, be telling. As the Italian oral historian Portelli argued, "[e]rrors, inventions and myths lead us through and beyond facts to their meanings".[36] Interviews suggest which sites of social infrastructure were significant enough to want to discuss in the present; interviewees are able to describe not simply what institutions existed but how individuals interacted with them; for instance, helping to establish the gendered patterns of the use of social infrastructure, and changing meanings given to "community". Findings from oral history interviews, as well as providing vivid first-hand testimony of life in the village going back to the 1950s, also allowed us to calibrate the cartographical presentation of social infrastructure in the village.

Focus groups are uncommonly used in urban and regional studies, although they have been used in political analyses of phenomena such as the "Red Wall".[37] They seem appropriate, however, as part of suite of mixed methods for the purposes of our research. Focus groups are a communicative tool for generating data. That is, social facts—replete with nuance in speech acts and an awareness of interpretation in exchanges—are not observable in one-on-one exchange and have been considered hard to replicate authentically online. The key premise is that researchers need to hear people responding to others, so as to know what is understood. Focus groups allow access to the language currently in use by the speakers to express things in context, although a task for researchers is to translate this into the language of others. Focus groups are used to get close to the subject matter and seek out diversity, description and depth in the data. The "thematic" approach to analysis draws out understandings and reasoning. Membership of the focus groups was recruited using purposive sampling. (Recruits were offered expenses, but all declined, and the researchers donated funds to the local foodbank instead.)

We undertook focus groups with three categories of producers and users of social infrastructure. The first was with representatives of agencies present in the village that engage with or provide social infrastructure. A second group included those active in the remaking of social infrastructure through community activity. Although discussion in these groups overlapped, an important broad difference emerged in the narratives in the two groups. Among the representative of the agencies, the key theme was the severe and intractable nature of the social problems in the village. Among those who lived there and were engaged in maintaining or rebuilding social infrastructure, while social problems were acknowledged, the emphasis was on the intense local attachments they felt and how this shaped their involvement in the remaking of social infrastructure. A third focus group was held with schoolchildren from Sacriston at a local secondary school. The voice of children is rarely heard in debates about urban and regional development, but this, surely, is a mistake as they will inherit the world we are discussing and making and, it turns out, have strong and clear views.

Finally, we undertook semi-structured interviews with actors who take a contemporary leading role in the production and maintenance of social infrastructure in the village. While this method is tried and tested as a means of gathering data in urban and regional studies, we have deployed it differently in this study. As well as gathering "facts", these interviews seek to understand the motivations, aspirations and life experiences of actors in the village. These interviews lasted up to two hours. The term "left behind places" already risks becoming a political stereotype, with the implication that such communities are homogenous and identical. Among other things, these interviews reveal the complexity of village life, the social changes underway there and the ways these are perceived.

3.5 A NARRATIVE OF CHANGE

The methods we employ in this study are not in themselves new, but we combine them here in a novel way and apply them to the question of the making, unmaking and remaking of social infrastructure in "left behind places" in ways that have not been previously attempted. The multiple methods and the size of team, comprising embedded and external researchers and those participating in the associational life of the village, allow us to triangulate our findings and continually assess the veracity and objectivity of our findings. Rarely, if ever, have these methods been applied in urban and regional studies, so we seek to demonstrate their value in this study, not least for informing policy. We offer additional perspectives and pathways for reading and analysing places, and, in particular, places outside of the spectrum targeted by conventional development flows such as "left behind" places. We emphasise the value of these methods in a field increasingly dominated by big data science. Our extended case method allows us to view the making, unmaking and remaking social infrastructure at different scales of action by private, state and community actors over time, grasping motivations and feelings, unearthing conflicts and progress. Finally, this is not an attempt to claim that the current and previous ways of researching and analysing places have no merit. Instead, this research aims to add layers of understanding to unpack and grasp the level of complexity that makes places. No one methodology can be all-encompassing and flawless. We can only strive to better understand the needs of people and their communities and aim at understanding what it means to have a basic level of well-being and quality of life. Only then can strategies be developed to provide endogenous and exogenous tools to address urban and regional inequalities. The methods used in this research, therefore, are qualitative and designed to elicit experiences and views and significance "in context". This means that validity is a matter of "authenticity", where the research seeks to build as complete and close a picture of a phenomenon as possible, in the case the making, unmaking and remaking of social infrastructure in a former mining village in County Durham.

NOTES

1 Local Trust (2019) *Left Behind? Understanding Communities on the Edge*. London: Local Trust. https://localtrust.org.uk/wp-content/uploads/2019/08/local_trust_ocsi_left_behind_research_august_2019.pdf
2 Martin R, Gardiner B, Pike A, Sunley P and Tyler P (2022) *Levelling Up Left Behind Places. The Scale and Nature of the Economic and Policy Challenge*. London: Taylor & Francis. https://doi.org/10.4324/9781032244341
3 Local Trust (2019), p 6.
4 Andrew Sayer (1992) *Method in Social Science. A Realist Approach*. London: Routledge.
5 We adapt this term from the literature on remote sensing, where ground truthing refers to the verification of image interpretation by direct observation of the ground; Michael Allaby (ed.) (2020) *A Dictionary of Geology and Earth Sciences*, 5th ed. Oxford: Oxford University Press.
6 Pike A, Béal V, Cauchi-Duval N, Franklin R, Kinossian N, Lang T, Leibert T, MacKinnon D, Rousseau M, Royer J, Servillo L, Tomaney J and Velthuis S (2022) "Left behind places": A geographical etymology. *Regional Studies*. https://doi.org/10.1080/00343404.2023.2167972
7 Dewey J (1927) *The Public and Its Problems*, New York, NY: Henry Holt, at 206.
8 Brandom R (2009) When pragmatism paints its blue on grey: Irony and the pragmatist enlightenment. In C Kautzer and E A Mendieta (eds.), *Pragmatism, Nation, Race*. Bloomington, IN: Indiana University Press, at 25. https://www.jstor.org/stable/j.ctt1dfnt09.5
9 Wills J and Lake R W (eds.) (2021) *The Power of Pragmatism. Knowledge Production and Social Inquiry*. Manchester: Manchester University Press. https://www.jstor.org/stable/j.ctv11vc913
10 There are historical models for this orientation to inquiry, such as the establishment of Hull House in Chicago in 1889 by Jane Addams and Ellen Gates Star, which was a focus for the study of poor neighbourhoods. This involved working with local communities to map social conditions and

provide evidence for social reform; Addams J (1910) *Twenty Years at Hull House*. New York, NY: Macmillan; Wade L C (1967) The heritage from Chicago's early settlement houses. *Journal of the Illinois State Historical Society*, 60(4): 411–441.

11 For an account of this early stage of the research, see Tomaney J, Natarajan L and Sutcliffe-Braithwate F (2021) Sacriston: Towards a deeper understanding of place. https://www.ucl.ac.uk/bartlett/planning/sites/bartlett/files/sacriston_report_2021_final.pdf

12 Star S L (1999) The ethnography of infrastructure. *American Behavioral Scientist*, 43(3): 377–391. https://doi.org/10.1177/00027649921955326

13 Koster M (2020) An ethnographic perspective on urban planning in Brazil: Temporality, diversity and critical urban theory. *International Journal of Urban and Regional Research*, 44(2): 185–199, at 197. https://doi.org/10.1111/1468-2427.12765

14 Mattilaa H, Olsson P, Lappid T-R and Ojanen K (2022) Ethnographic knowledge in urban planning—Bridging the gap between the theories of knowledge-based and communicative planning. *Planning Theory and Practice*, 23(1): 11–25. https://doi.org/10.1080/14649357.2021.1993316

15 Hall S M (2020) Social reproduction as social infrastructure. *Soundings*, 76: 82–94. https://doi.org/10.3898/SOUN.76.06.2020

16 Frankenberg R (1957) *Village on the Border: A Social Study of Religion, Politics and Football in a North Wales Community*. London: Cohen & West.

17 Gluckman M (1957), "Preface", in Frankenberg (1957), at 3, see Reference 16.

18 Burawoy (1998) The extended case method. *Sociological Theory*, 16(1): 4–33, at 5. https://doi.org/10.1111/0735-2751.00040

19 Flyvbjerg B (2006) Five misunderstandings about case-study research. *Qualitative Inquiry*, 12(2): 219–125. https://doi.org/10.1177/1077800405284363

20 Burawoy et al. (2000) *Global Ethnography. Forces, Connections, and Imaginations in a Postmodern World*. Berkeley, CA: University of California Press.

21 See chapter 4 for a discussion of the Durham Miners' Association.

22 Wills J (2012) The geography of community and political organisation in London today. *Political Geography*, 31(2): 120. https://doi.org/10.1016/j.polgeo.2011.11.003

23 Klinenberg E (2020) *Palaces for People. How to Build a More Equal and United Society*. London: Vintage, at 151.

24 Brewer J and Hunter A (1989). *Multimethod Research: A Synthesis of Styles*. Thousand Oaks, CA: Sage; Burke Johnson R and Onwuegbuzle A (2004) Mixed methods research: A research paradigm whose time has come. *Educational Researcher*, 33(7): 14–26. https://doi.org/10.3102/0013189X033007014

25 Bryman A (2006) Integrating quantitative and qualitative research: How is it done? *Qualitative Research*, 6(1): 97–113. https://doi.org/10.1177/1468794106058877; Pike A, MacKinnon D, Cumbers A, Dawley S and McMaster R (2016) Doing evolution in economic geography. *Economic Geography*, 92(2): 123–144. https://doi.org/10.1080/00130095.2015.1108830

26 Giddens A (1990) *The Constitution of Society; Outline of the Theory of Structuration*. Cambridge: Polity, at 80.

27 Hebbert M (2016) Figure-ground: History and practice of a planning technique. *Town Planning Review*, 87(6): 705–728. https://doi.org/10.3828/tpr.2016.44; Trancik R. (1986). *Finding Lost Space: Theories of Urban Design*. New York, NY: Van Nostrand Reinhold.

28 Barnes T (2021) Rorty, conversation and the power of maps. In Wills J and Lake R W (eds.), *The Power of Pragmatism. Knowledge Production and Social Inquiry*. Manchester: Manchester University Press. https://doi.org/10.7765/9781526134950.00012

29 Ross T and Stoddart A (1921) *Jubilee History of Annfield Plan Industrial Cooperative Society Ltd, 1870–1920*. Manchester: Co-operative Wholesale Printing Works.

30 Lenders J (1930) *History of the Parish of Sacriston*. Bruges: Gruuthuuse.

31 Fenn L A (1924) County Organisation—Durham. *The Labour Woman*, 1 August; Gibb M (1945) *Durham County Labour Women's Advisory Council: Silver Jubilee, 1920–1945*. Durham: Redhills Miners' Hall.

32 Oxley J (1924) *The Birth of a Movement. A Tribute the Memory of Joseph Hopper*. Gateshead: Gateshead District Aged Mineworkers Homes; House of Commons (1899) *Second Special Report and Report from the Select Committee on The Cottage Homes Bill, Together with The Proceedings of the Committee, Minutes of Evidence, and Appendix*. Ordered, by The House of Commons, to be Printed, 7th July. London: HMSO, Evidence of Joseph Hopper, pp 117–124; Durham Aged Mineworkers' Homes Association (1909) *An Appreciation of the Life of Joseph Hopper. Pioneer of the Durham Aged Mineworkers' Homes Association*. Durham.

33 Chapman J (2003) *Cream Teas and Nutty Slack. A History of Club Cricket in County Durham, 1751–2002*. Chester-le-Street: privately published.

34 Lawson J (1936) *Peter Lee*. London: Epworth.

35 Rand D and Claughan L (2002) *Sacriston Workmens Club, 1902–2002. A Centenary Souvenir*. Privately published.

36 Portelli A (1991) *The Death of Luigi Trastulli and Other Stories: Form and Meaning in Oral History*. Albany, NY: State University of New York Press, at 2.

37 Broadly, the "Red Wall" refers to parliamentary constituencies in "left behind places" in the UK that traditional voted Labour but switched to the Conservatives in the 2019 General Election; Mattinson D (2020) *Beyond the Red Wall: Why Labour Lost, How the Conservatives Won and What Will Happen Next?* London: Biteback.

4. Political economy of Sacriston

Keywords: Sacriston; coal mining; deindustrialisation; community

The focus of this study is the making, unmaking and remaking of social infrastructure in "left behind places". In chapter 2, we argued for moving beyond a view of "left behind places" as aggregates of statistics and accumulations of human capital and, instead, presented them as "moral communities". With this in mind, in chapter 3 we proposed a set of mixed methods to allow us to develop a "deep place" account of the development of social infrastructure, presented in the form of a historical narrative. In this chapter, we outline the (changing) wider political and economic context in which social infrastructure was made, unmade and remade. Sacriston owes its existence to coal and the rise and fall of the industry, and the policy responses to this is the backdrop to our story. A discussion of this wider context is often missing in contemporary discussion of social infrastructure but is crucial to our understanding. This chapter briefly explains this larger story as it pertains to development in Sacriston. The Appendix provides a timeline of key events in the village.

Sacriston was a handful of farms in the parish of Witton Gilbert until the sinking of the colliery in 1839. By 1850, the rudiments of a village were visible on the Ordnance Survey map. Constructing historic population data at the scale of Sacriston is challenging, but we offer some estimates to help contextualise later developments. The population grew rapidly during the second half of the 19th century as the coal industry expanded and peaked in 1921, around the time that output in the coalfield reached its zenith (Figure 4.1). Migrants were drawn from far afield, attracted by employment opportunities, but also responding to push factors, such as the shrinkage of agricultural workforce elsewhere in Britain, or famine in Ireland.

Figure 4.1 Population change in Witton Gilbert Parish, 1841–1921

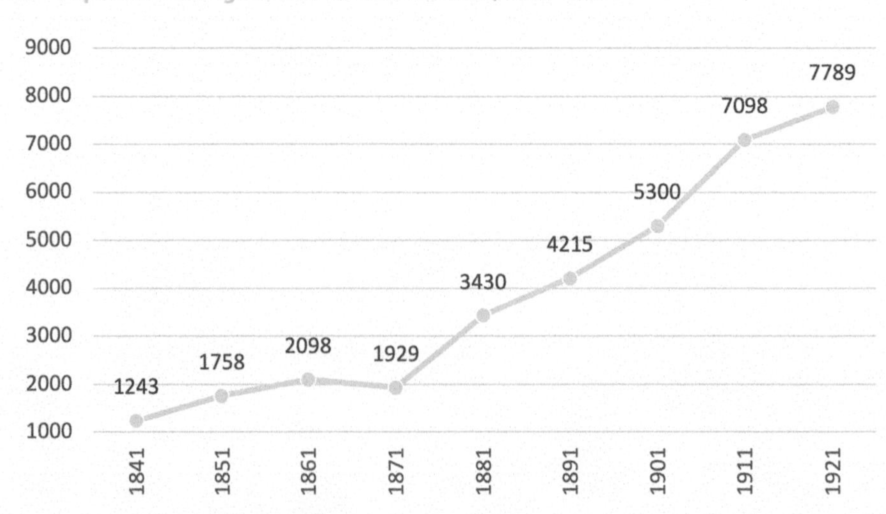

Sources: Population data sourced from the Census: Office for National Statistics (https://www.ons.gov.uk); NOMIS (https://www.nomisweb.co.uk); and Histpop (http://www.histpop.org) (accessed 15 June 2022)

https://doi.org/10.1080/2578711X.2023.2254999

Figure 4.2 Population change in Sacriston Parish, 1921–2011

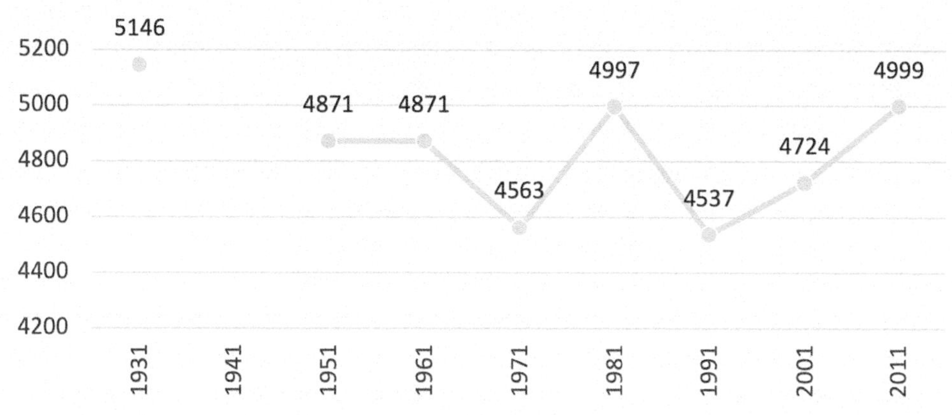

Sources: Population data sourced from the Census: Office for National Statistics (https://www.ons.gov.uk); NOMIS (https://www.nomisweb.co.uk); and Histpop (http://www.histpop.org) (accessed 15 June 2022)

Population growth was arrested after the First World War, when the coal industry and the wider regional economy entered a crisis. This was a period of substantial outmigration from the Durham coalfield in the direction of the South and Midlands and further afield, which offered employment opportunities in emerging industries such car manufacturing and consumer goods production.[1] From 1931, we are able more easily to chart Sacriston's development because it was separated from the wider Witton Gilbert parish in 1937, when it became a parish in its own right. Population fell during the interwar period. There was no census in 1941, but by 1951 the population had not returned to its 1921 level (Figure 4.2 and Table 4.1).

Table 4.1 Population change (percentage points) per decade (a) compared with the previous decade and (b) compared with 1921, the year when Sacriston recorded its highest population

Date	Population	(a) Decade change	(b) Population compared with 1921
1921	5973		
1931	5146	−16%	−16%
1941[a]	–	–	–
1951	4871	−6%	−23%
1961	4871	0%	−23%
1971	4563	−7%	−31%
1981	4997	+9%	−20%
1991	4537	−10%	−32%
2001	4724	+4%	−26%
2011	4999	+6%	−19%

Sources: Population data sourced from the Census: Office for National Statistics (https://www.ons.gov.uk); NOMIS (https://www.nomisweb.co.uk); and Histpop (http://www.histpop.org) (accessed 15 June 2022)
Note: [a]There was no 1941 census due to the Second World War.

The key driver of population growth before 1921 was the demand for labour in the expanding coal industry. Sacriston Colliery was owned by the Charlaw and Sacriston Collieries Co. Ltd before 1947, which also operated other mines nearby at Kimblesworth, Nettlesworth and Witton. Employment at Sacriston Colliery grew rapidly in the second half of the 19th century, peaking in 1929, when 966 men worked at the pit. Before 1947, although the numbers officially employed were high, work was not always certain. The late 19th century was a period of exceptional economic growth and rising real wages, but this growth was episodic and uneven. When the demand for coal fell, the reaction of employers typically was immediately to seek wage cuts or lay off workers. As well as reducing household incomes, this shaped the development of social infrastructure. Fr. Lenders, in his account of the early life of the Catholic parish in Sacriston, reports how efforts to repay the debts incurred in building St Bede's Catholic Church—and to pay the parish priest's stipend—were setback by the social and economic conflicts of the period:

> Several times during Fr. Gillow's pastorate, his work and the readiness of his congregation were hampered by lack of labour or strikes; in 1893 we see that Fr. Gillow had no support for 14 weeks and had to assist members of the congregation to a great extent.[2]

Such conditions were the background to the struggle to create a trade union, culminating in the formation of the Durham Miner's Association in 1869, which fought to improve conditions at the workplace. After the First World War, general economic conditions deteriorated, meaning that short-time working was a regular occurrence and Sacriston pit stood idle at times. Reflecting on her life in a Northumberland pit village around this time, Linda McCullough Thew writes:

> The pit was dark, solid and forever. It supplied the money on which the community relied. Yet it was a fickle master. My father, being a safety man, worked regularly, but, for many of the others a full week's work was by no means a certainty.[3]

The coal industry was nationalised in 1947. This was a longstanding demand of the Miners' Federation of Great Britain (the National Union of Mineworkers from 1947). Following nationalisation, in Sacriston, employment remained high during the 1940s and 1950s, reflecting the demands of war production and post-war reconstruction. This was also a period during which the welfare state was expanding. In general, this was an era of rising living standards and also some improvements in working conditions as the state expanded its re-distributional role. In County Durham, the extent of direct government control over swathes of industry rendered it, according to Hudson, a "state-manged region".[4] The Attlee Labour government of 1945 was concerned with national "productionism"—with the building of a British-focused economy, coupled with a renewed warfare state.[5]

The Durham Miner's Association reached the zenith of its political power in the two decades after the Second World war. Vast crowds attended the annual Durham Miners' Gala, which became a state occasion for the British labour movement, attracting national and international political leaders to witness the spectacle.[6] In her memoir, which partly recounts growing up in the Durham coalfield, Hill notes that, "In the 1950s, the Durham miners thought they had made it."[7] But there was a cost to these gains, notably in the form of a seepage of social and economic control away from the village. This was the era of what Scott calls "high modernism", in which centralised technical expertise and reasoned knowledge trumped local experience as the solutions to social problems. Under these conditions, "Officials of the modern state are, of necessity, at least one—and often several steps—removed from the society they are charged with governing."[8] This distancing of (local) state and community had implications for the fate of social infrastructure in later decades.

Intimations of a more challenging future were apparent early on in the post-war period, moreover, as the prospects of a post-coal economy began to form. In 1951, Durham County Council published its Development Plan, which looked forward to an era with a substantially smaller coal industry. All settlements in the county were placed in one of four categories: Category A, where the population was likely to increase and would be a focus for capital investment; Category B, where population would be stable; and Category C, where population was expected to decline, and investment would be limited. Places allocated to Category D included:

> Those from which a considerable loss of population may be expected. In these cases it is felt that there should be no further investment of capital on any considerable scale, and that any proposal to invest capital should be carefully examined. This generally means that when the existing houses become uninhabitable they should be replaced elsewhere, and that any expenditure on facilities and services in these communities which would involve public money should be limited to conform to what appears to be the possible future life of existing property in the community.... There is no proposal to demolish any village, nor is there a policy against genuine village life. It is proposed to remould gradually the pattern of development in the interests of the county as a whole.[9]

Category D villages were concentrated in the west of County Durham where most mine closures were anticipated, because coal seams there were thin and unsuitable for mechanisation and pits costly to operate. In 1951, 114 settlements were listed as Category D; this number rose to 121 in the revised Durham County Development Plan of 1964. These areas received no investment for 26 years until the policy ended in 1977.[10] A significant amount of social infrastructure was lost across County Durham during this period, often in the face of community opposition, casting a new light on the nature of "left behindness", which from this perspective has been in the making for generations. Arguably, then, parts of County Durham have been "left behind" for generations.

Sacriston was allocated to Category A, which meant it would be a focus for investment in infrastructure and services, reflecting the relatively positive outlook for employment at the colliery at that time. But adjacent settlements, however, such as Edmondsley, Waldridge, Nettlesworth and Kimblesworth, were assigned to Category D. Today all are substantially smaller in population terms than they were 60 years ago. The hamlet of Hamsteels, 6.5 km from Sacriston along the Browney Valley, was completely erased as a result of the Category D policy.[11] This broad thrust in the development of the county was reinforced in 1963 by the publication of the Hailsham Plan, named for the Conservative minister who oversaw its publication. It set out a vision of North East England in which population and economic activity would be concentrated near the east coast, where the most productive pits were located and where infrastructure and labour, including New Towns, could be assembled that might prove attractive to mobile investors.[12] During the 1960s and 1970s, therefore, the social and economic geography of County Durham was reshaped in in significant ways as a result of national and local public policy.

Shifting energy policies accelerated the contraction of the Durham coalfield in the 1960s. The arrival of oil and nuclear power marginalised coal in the energy mix. In 1959, the Durham coalfield still employed 93,000 miners, but by 1974 this number had fallen to 27,000.[13] Widespread colliery closures were enacted. Sacriston Colliery survived this cull, but by 1960, employment had fallen to around 500 from its peak of 950 in the inter-war period. In part, this was result of the mechanisation of mining, which improved the productivity of remaining pits. The pit survived also because it mined high-quality coking coal that was a critical input to steelmaking. After 1974, the long-term contraction of the coalfield was arrested by the rapid rise in oil prices, which offered a reprieve to the industry. But in the 1980s, intensifying deindustrialisation of British industry threatened the future of the colliery and it was slated for closure several times. By the time the colliery closed in 1985, in the immediate aftermath of the 1984/85 miners' strike, only 300 men were employed there.[14]

Coal mine closures in the 1960s occurred in a context when other sectors in the regional economy were expanding. The growth of public and private services and a large expansion of regional policy to attract new manufacturing industries helped mitigated the effects of coal mine closure, even if the transition was not always straightforward.[15] The National Coal Board, at times, opposed new inward investment if it threatened to attract men away from mining jobs. The closure of Sacriston Colliery occurred in different circumstances from the mass closures of the 1960s. Job losses now were occurring across the economy, including in the public sector and among inward investors who had arrived in the 1960s and 1970s.

The provision of social infrastructure occurs within the context of broader social and economic changes in Sacriston and County Durham described in this chapter. The making of social infrastructure emerged from intense social and economic struggles, but occurred in the context of an expanding coalfield. After the Second World War, County Durham was incorporated into a "state managed region" and control of the local economy and social infrastructure began to slip away from the village. This was a long and uneven process, although it accelerated following the closure of the colliery and the decade of austerity after 2010. We flesh out this story in the following chapters.

NOTES

1 Scott P (1999) The state, internal migration, and the growth of new industrial communities in inter-war Britain. *English Historical Review*, 115(125): 329–353. https://doi.org/10.1093/ehr/115.461.329

2 Lenders J (1930) *History of the Parish of Sacriston*. Bruges: Gruuthuuse, at 48.

3 McCullough Thew L (1985) *The Pit Village and the Store. The Portrait of a Mining Past*. London: Pluto, at 68–69.

4 Hudson R (1989) *Wrecking a Region. State Policies, Party Politics and Regional Change in North East England*. London: Pion.

5 Edgerton D (2008) *The Rise and Fall of the British Nation*. London: Penguin.

6 Tomaney J (2020) After coal: Meanings of the Durham Miners' Gala. *Frontiers in Sociology*, 5(32). https://doi.org/10.3389/fsoc.2020.00032

7 Hill F (2021) *There is Nothing for You Here: Finding Opportunity in the Twenty-First Century*. Boston, MA: Mariner, at 25.

8 Scott J (1999) *Seeing Like a State: How Certain Schemes to Improve the Human Condition Have Failed*. London & New Haven, CT: Yale University Press.

9 Durham County Council (1951) *County Development Plan [1951]: Written Statement*. Durham: Durham County Council.

10 Pattinson G (2004) Planning for decline: The "D"-village policy of County Durham, UK. *Planning Perspectives*, 19(3): 311–332. https://doi.org/10.1080/02665430410001709804

11 Coster G (1990) Death of a hamlet. *The Guardian*, 24–25 February, pp. 17–22.

12 Board of Trade (1963) *The North East: A Programme for Regional Development* (Cmd 2206). London: HMSO.

13 Hudson (1989), see Reference 4.

14 See http://www.dmm.org.uk/colliery/s019.htm

15 Department of Employment and Productivity (1970) *Ryhope: A Pit Closes. A Study in Redeployment*. London: HMSO.

5. Moral community: the making of social infrastructure in Sacriston

Keywords: Sacriston; moral community; social infrastructure; place attachments

In chapter 2 we made the case for left behind places as moral communities and presented the making, unmaking and remaking social infrastructure as an expression of this. We set out our approach to the study of these processes in the form of a deep-place study of one village. In the previous chapter we sketched the historical context in which social infrastructure was produced and maintained. This chapter seeks to understand how Sacriston came to be richly endowed with social infrastructure in the period before the Second World War. Reflecting our aim of deepening our understanding of the processes at work, and deploying the methods described in chapter 3, we draw primarily on archival sources. This account shows that the making of social infrastructure was mainly the product of efforts of people in the village, funded largely from their own resources, mainly contributions from households, supported on occasion by gifts from the Charlaw and Sacriston Collieries Company. The making of this social infrastructure was typically in intergenerational process and achieved in the context of the difficulties posed by the political and economic context but aimed at meeting the pressing human needs described in chapter 3. Sacriston was founded as a "moral community", in the famous formulation of the Welsh writer and novelist, Raymond Williams, rooted in values that emphasised "neighbourhood, mutual obligation, and common betterment".[1]

In 1839, a shaft was sunk and a colliery established in fields below Sacriston Heugh in the parish of Witton Gilbert 5 km north of Durham City. By 1850, Sacriston was established as a small village, comprising a handful of insanitary and overcrowded terraced cottages—the "Cross Streets"—hastily erected by the coal company to accommodate its new workforce. Migrants flocked to take advantage of the new employment opportunities in the mines. A new world was being thrown together at the leading edge of global capitalism and a wave of social infrastructure-building began in the mining villages of County Durham, in large part organised and resourced by miners and their families themselves via their collective associations. The creation of social infrastructure was contested and created exclusions as well as inclusions. Religious buildings catered to segregated communities. Access to social infrastructure was also highly gendered in a society focused on an industry that employed an exclusively male workforce. Nevertheless, as the Durham miner, turned writer, Sid Chaplin, put it, "each village was, in fact, a sort of self-constructed, do-it-yourself counter-environment. … The people had built it themselves".[2] In his book about the pseudonymous Durham mining village, "East Tanthope",[3] published in 1946, the American sociologist Mark Benney noted:

> wherever, by chance, the eye rests upon some building more attractive than its neighbors, one almost invariably finds that it owes its existence to the organized efforts of the miners themselves. Their clubs, welfare institutes, and co-op stores are outstanding institutional buildings. … Nothing has come easily to this village. When it felt a need, it had tried to supply it for itself, and if anyone opposed the effort, the village had fought. Every institution in the village with the exception of the cinema, the post-office and the church, the people had built themselves or struggled for through their union.[4]

https://doi.org/10.1080/2578711X.2023.2255000

To begin with, Sacriston, like other coalfield villages, lacked basic infrastructure and services. Water and sanitation provision comprised, at best, standpipes and dry closets, while roads were unpaved and street lighting non-existent. Medical provision was rudimentary. The earliest social infrastructure came in the form of religious institutions and buildings. By 1890, as attested by business directories, villagers had built Wesleyan and Primitive Methodist chapels, a Catholic Church—to accommodate Irish migrants—and an Anglican Church. Later, other Methodist sects built chapels, along with Plymouth Brethren, while the Salvation Army opened a citadel in the village. These were not simply places of Christian worship but were also centres for social action. The Anglicans and Catholics built schools, while a Sunday School tradition developed among the Methodists. Alongside religious buildings, a working men's club opened in 1902.[5] Almost all this social infrastructure was funded from resources generated within the village itself. The village also contained several pubs, which provided opportunities mainly for men to socialise outside the home. The village hosted a vibrant sporting life. For instance, Sacriston Colliery Cricket Club was established in 1874 and soon joined the local league in order to be able to compete with neighbouring villages (Figure 5.1).[6]

Conditions in both the mine and the village were harsh. Although Sacriston largely avoided the major underground disasters experienced by some nearby villages, mining work was difficult, dirty, dangerous and periodically deadly. Major strikes, above all, in 1926, caused immense hardship. The leadership of the Durham Miners' Association (DMA) pursued a distinctive politics of moderation and conciliation with the owners through most of this period. Local branches of the union ("Lodges") became increasingly important in the workplace where strong traditions of solidarity developed, and in village life where the Lodge became involved in the battle to improve social conditions. Lodge banners, paraded most regularly at the annual Durham Miners' Gala, were treated with reverence and became symbols of village identity.[7] While the focus of this chapter is the making of social infrastructure, it is important to bear in mind that the Lodge remained the most important institution in the village during this period.[8]

Religious institutions—churches and chapels—were among the earliest forms of social infrastructure and were at the heart of village life for several generations. A Primitive Methodist chapel is marked on an 1857 Ordnance Survey map. It was later replaced by a larger chapel. Primitive Methodists played a disproportionate role in the social and political development of the Durham coalfield in the 19th century.[9] William Crawford, appointed secretary of the DMA in 1863, his successor William Patterson and, later, his successor John Wilson were all Primitive Methodists. The Labour leader of Durham County Council in the interwar period, Peter Lee, was also a Primitive Methodist. Many of the founders of Lodges were Primitive Methodists or linked to other Methodist sects such as the Wesleyans or New Connexion. Methodism only ever attracted a minority of the population in mining villages, but it supplied

Figure 5.1 Social infrastructure in Sacriston, County Durham, 1910

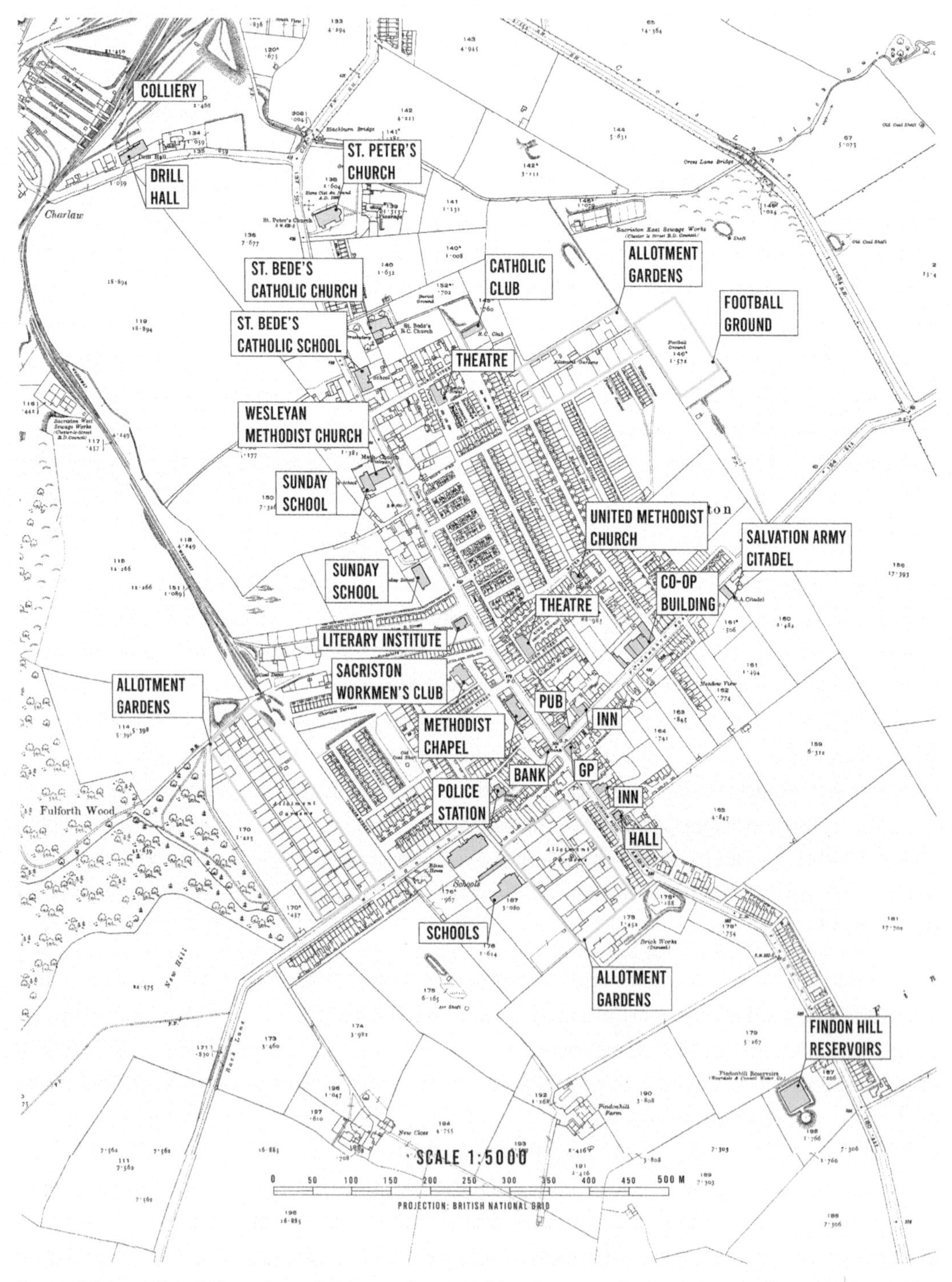

Sources: Digimap Historic Roam, https://digimap.edina.ac.uk/historic, accessed 1 October 2021; adapted by the authors
Note: Scale 1:5000

a disproportionate share of leaders and a "penumbra" of people who were not registered members but participated in the activities of the chapels, such as concerts and outings. The building of chapels often was supported by employers—for instance, through bequests of land—and some colliery owners and managers were Methodists themselves.[10] In Sacriston, Alderman T. F. Brass, OBE, deputy manager of the colliery in the first decades of the 20th century, was a prominent Wesleyan preacher and a leading promoter of temperance in the village, responsible for organising "Pleasant Sunday Afternoons"—activities designed to keep miners out of pubs. The Methodist chapel was a place where employer and worker met on equal terms outside the mine.

The building of St Bede's Catholic Church is another early and informative episode of social infrastructure-making in Sacriston. County Durham was a major centre of mass Irish immigration in the 19th century.[11] Fr. Lenders, writing in 1930, was able to draw upon living memory to develop an early account of the Irish experience in Sacriston. Irish immigration began in the 1850s when a "great number of Irishmen haunted by famine" made the journey from Galway to Sacriston.[12] Very quickly, a Gaelic-speaking community formed in the Cross Streets. Irish immigrants faced sectarianism; according to Lenders, "they were considered as belonging to a race altogether inferior".[13] Catholics would gather at Findon Hill for protection before walking as a group to mass in Durham. Sectarian tensions could boil over into violence:

> On the pay Friday, the poor Irishmen went to drown the sorrows of their exile in a pint of beer; then, with their natural excitability, when some words were said against the Catholic Religion, Our Lady, their priests or Ireland, fists and sticks came into action: a mêlée ensued.[14]

A Catholic Mission was established in Sacriston in 1867 and an Irish-born Gaelic-speaking priest was appointed to lead it. A rudimentary Catholic school was fashioned from two adjoining miners' cottages and enrolments rose, even if attendance was intermittent. Fund-raising began among Irish miners to build a Catholic church and Presbytery. Construction was underway by 1878, but halted when funds ran out. The church was completed in 1881 and named after a local, Northumbrian saint, Bede. The following year a Catholic cemetery was opened and, in 1894, a purpose-built Catholic school was completed. In 1907, the "League Hall" was built to house the activities of the League of the Cross, a Catholic temperance movement. It became the location of the annual celebration of the Feast of St Patrick, the patron saint of Ireland, but also:

> a centre of the social activity of the congregation, in which would be found a billiard-table and several kinds of indoor games, a library of good and instructive books, a stage, etc. so that the congregation would have an always-ready and its-own place for meeting of the League, concerts, whist-drives, socials, lectures, tea-parties, meetings for special-purposes, etc.[15]

The clergy's efforts to limit drinking always failed and the hall was later converted to a Catholic Club that sold alcohol.

The Irish in Sacriston provide an example of determined social infrastructure-making with lasting effects. According to Fr. Lenders, building efforts were funded by "the pennies and sixpences collected one by one from house to house", supplemented by lotteries and tea-parties while, periodically, Catholic miners would contribute a day's wage.[16] Fr. Lenders imagines "an old Irish grannie" looking upon the new school and saying, "It is my school; some of the bricks have been paid for with my pennies."[17] While this was largely true, it was also the case the Charlaw and Sacriston Collieries Company gifted the land on which the church was built and donated to the costs of building the League Hall, and, in a demonstration of support, the colliery manager, W. C. Blackett, opened the leek show there in 1909. Overall, though, there is a strong sense of the making of social infrastructure was the outcome of efforts by the local community.

This religiously oriented social infrastructure might be seen to entrench religious rivalries. Certainly, Irish identity remained strong in the village, a branch of the Irish National League—which campaigned for Home Rule in Ireland—was formed in 1894.[18] But, by 1930, Fr. Lenders felt able to remark that Sacriston was now characterised by "toleration and kindness and sociability".[19] The integration of the Irish into village life was accelerated by the onset of the First World War. Two important episodes exemplify this. Irish miners from Sacriston volunteered in significant numbers to join the British Army, serving mainly in the Tyneside Irish Brigade, which suffered massive casualties at the Battle of the Somme in 1916.[20] The local press regularly reported the enlistment of men from the Sacriston Cross Streets.[21] Meanwhile, on the home front, the Catholic community in Sacriston raised £300 locally in order to cover the costs of housing Belgian refugees in the village, but it did so alongside Methodists, members of the Workmen's Club and others.[22] By the end of the First World War, the local press had stopped referring to Catholic miners as "Irishmen", although a branch of the Irish Self-Determination League—a nationalist movement—was formed in the village in the aftermath of the Easter Rising—the uprising against British rule in Ireland in 1916. This suggests old identities died slowly.[23]

In this milieu, local traditions of cooperation and mutualism were deepened. Two clear examples are provided by the village Co-op (or "Store", as it was universally known) and the Durham Aged Mineworkers' Homes Association (DAMHA). In 1897, the Annfield Plain Industrial Co-operative Society Ltd opened its fourth branch in Sacriston.[24] The society was one of several that had been formed across County Durham during last quarter of the 19th century to improve the quality of retail services available in villages.[25] While co-operative societies existed throughout Britain, County Durham had the highest membership rate in the country by 1940 (29%)—twice that of South East England.[26] (The rate of membership in Sacriston itself likely was higher still.) The society's profit—or "surplus", as it was known—was shared among the members in the form of a "Dividend", allocated in proportion to the amount the household had spent (Figure 5.2).

Figure 5.2 Sacriston branch of the Annfield Plain Industrial and Co-operative Society, *c.*1920

Source: Beamish Museum, NEG 183586

The opening of the Sacriston branch of the Co-op was a major event and contemporary reports lauded its opulence. *The Builder* reported:

> A branch of the Annfield Plain Cooperative Society was opened at Sacriston recently. There are five departments, with frontages to the Plawsworth Road, the whole extending to 200 ft. Over the shops is a hall providing accommodation for 700 persons, and behind is a yard with a manager's house, warehouses, slaughter house, stabling and other out-offices. The whole are built of stone. The building has been designed by GT Wilson of Blackhill and erected by T Hilton of Bishop Auckland, cost £5,000 to £6,000.[27]

The Store expanded over time to include departments for grocery and provisions, drapery, millinery, boots, hardware and furnishing, shoe repair, confectionary, greengrocery, and butchery.[28] On the first floor, the "Store Hall" became an important location for social and political activities. For instance, in 1917, a "grand concert" was held in the Cooperative Hall "for our Belgian friends".[29]

Linda McCullough Thew, who grew up in a mining village in the Northumberland coalfield and later worked in the local Co-op attested:

> My family, the church, the school, the pit and the store. These were woven into the fabric of my life from the beginning. Allegiance to the church might waver, schools change, our stay in various houses be short-lived, work at the pit be unpredictable but our attitude to the store was steadfast. It claimed our wholehearted fealty and esteem.[30]

The Store was a lynchpin of the community. During the 1926 strike, all Store members were given credit and allowed generous repayment terms in order to relieve the intense hardship being endured by local households. According to McCullough Thew, in some cases, these debts were eventually written off.

The DAMHA grew from the vision of Joseph Hopper, a miner, Methodist preacher and Durham County councillor, to meet the needs of miners and their families who otherwise would be evicted from tied colliery homes when they retired. Hopper was the first miner to be elected to the Gateshead Poor Law Guardians and saw the problem of destitute retired miners and their wives or widows ending up in the workhouse and began formulating the concept of collective housing provision for aged miners across County Durham.[31] A weekly levy voluntarily donated from miners' wages, plus donations of land and materials from mine owners and others, allowed houses to be constructed and let free of charge. Local committees of the DAMHA were formed in each village, including one in Sacriston, to raise funds and build aged miners' cottages (Figure 5.3). Similar levies were used to support the provision of a range of social infrastructure in the villages, such as miners' institutes.

Despite the social, industrial and political upheavals of the time, the 1920s saw an expansion of house building by the Association in County Durham. The first aged miners' homes in Sacriston were opened on Plawsworth Road, a short walk from the Co-op, in the midst of the 1926 Miners' Lockout and, perhaps surprisingly given the fraught political and industrial context, the opening was attended by the colliery management as well as union officials. The DAMHA was viewed, contemporaneously, as a central and prefigurative element of an emerging local tradition of mutualism and cooperation (Figure 5.4).

The Labour Party emerged in the first decade of 20th century as the vehicle to advance working-class interests in County Durham. Branches were formed across the county and long campaigns led the DMA to switch allegiance from the Liberals to Labour. A key moment occurred in the 1906 General Election when John Wilkinson Taylor, backed by the DMA, defeated both the Liberal and Conservative candidates, and was elected as Labour MP for the Chester-le-Street parliamentary constituency, of which Sacriston was part. In several respects, Taylor personified the constituency he represented. He was secretary of his Durham Colliery Mechanics Association Lodge before becoming secretary of the County Association in 1897. Alongside

Figure 5.3 Durham Aged Mineworkers' Homes Association, Sacriston Local Committee, 1928

Sacriston Aged Miners' Homes Local Committee, 1928. Back row, left to right: W. Alderton, S. Boswell, J. Britton, Rev T.H. Burnett, T. Holmes, J. Cuthbert, S. Greenwell. Front row: W. Bulmer, T. Futers, M. Lavelle, B. Lambert, J. Adair, J.R. Grossart, W. Todd, H. Snowball. Insets, left to right: W. Errington, T.F. Brass, W.B. Willis.

Source: Beamish Museum, NEG 84650

this, he was president of the Annfield Plain Industrial and Cooperative Society, a county councillor, an urban district councillor, chairman of the DAMHA and a founder of the Independent Labour Party. And, of course, he was a Primitive Methodist preacher.[32]

Labour has represented the constituency uninterrupted, in its various guises, since then. At a local scale, Labour also began to win representation on parish and district councils and boards of Poor Law Guardians. In 1919, Labour won control of Durham County Council. After briefly losing its majority, Labour recaptured the county council in 1923. It presided over major social advances, including the management of hospitals and the creation of a public health system that led to rapid reductions in child mortality,[33] while Labour-controlled Chester-le-Street Rural District Council built council houses at twice the national rate, consolidating the party's hegemony.[34] Labour from 1906 onwards provided the connective tissue that linked political, industrial and social action.[35] The relative strength of local government, and its control by Labour organically linked to the local community, provided enabling conditions for the making of social infrastructure. But although Sacriston remains represented by Labour in parliament and on the council, after a century, Labour lost control of Durham County Council in

Figure 5.4 Aged Miners' Homes, Sacriston, opened 1926

Source: Beamish Museum, NEG 84649

2021, an event which has been explained in the context of a broader loss of electoral support in its "heartlands" or the "Red Wall".[36]

The making of social infrastructure during this period was a highly gendered process. Men dominated the leadership of the Methodist chapels, the Co-op and the DAMHA district committees, and women were actively excluded from some aspects of social infrastructure, such as the Workmen's Club. But his does not mean women were absent from the efforts to build social infrastructure. On the contrary, through organisations such the Catholic Women's League of the Cross, Women's Cooperative Guild and, especially, the Women's Sections of the Labour Party, women were socially and politically active, if marginalised.[37] Although often operating in auxiliary capacity, women were far more present that conventional accounts suggest. Moreover, Sacriston produced during this period one the outstanding political leaders of interwar County Durham, Annie Errington, a Sacriston miners' wife. She was 38 years old before she could vote or hold elected office, following the expansion of the franchise in 1918. But, by 1925, she had been elected to Chester-le-Street Rural District Council. She was a leader of the Labour Party Women's Section, a mass movement of miners' wives in County Durham, that could mobilise thousands of women

Figure 5.5 Sacriston Labour Party Women's Section, probably at the Durham Miners' Gala, 1939

Source: Beamish Museum, NEG 29195

and which organised political education for hundreds of them (Figure 5.5). Errington was among the members of the Chester-le-Street Poor Law Guardians Board who were surcharged and threatened with gaol for the welfare payments they made to striking miners in 1926. Also in 1926, she was part of a delegation of miners' wives that travelled to Russia to meet Soviet trade unions, where she addressed a meeting of 5000 Red Army soldiers. A lifelong Wesleyan Methodist and member of the Co-operative Women's Guild, she was appointed a magistrate in 1938. Errington was an exceptional figure who, nevertheless, personifies the social and political activism that shaped Durham mining villages during this period.[38]

The making of social infrastructure during this period was a struggle marked by setbacks as well as progress, but, by 1925, Sacriston was bestowed with a wide and diverse range of social infrastructure, largely produced people in the village itself. It involved generational commitments and helped produce the distinctive identity of the village, paraded, literally, behind the Lodge band and banner annually at the Durham Miners' Gala.[39] At heart of the village was the mine and the Lodge, and later the Labour Party, and these provided the connective tissue that linked the various efforts to make social infrastructure. Sacriston was constructed as a "moral community", founded on distinctive—if imperfect—values.

NOTES

1 Williams R (1989) *Resources of Hope. Culture, Democracy, Socialism*. London: Verso, at 96.

2 Chaplin S (1978) Durham mining villages. In M Bulmer (ed.), *Mining and Social Change. Durham County in the Twentieth Century*, at 80–81. London: Croom Helm.

3 It is not certain to which actual village Benney refers, but the most likely candidate is East Stanley, about 9 km from Sacriston.

4 Benney M (1946) *Charity Main A Coalfield Chronicle*. London: G. Allen & Unwin, at 162.

5 Rand D and Claughan L (2002) *Sacriston Workmens Club, 1902–2002. A Centenary Souvenir*. Privately published.

6 Chapman J (2003) *Cream Teas and Nutty Slack. A History of Club Cricket in County Durham, 1751–2002*. Chester-le-Street: privately published.

7 Tomaney J (2020) After coal: Meanings of the Durham Miners' Gala. *Frontiers of Sociology*, 5(32): 13. https://doi.org/10.3389/fsoc.2020.00032

8 Brown K (1987) The lodges of the Durham Miners' Association, 1869–1926. *Northern History*, 23(1): 138–152. https://doi.org/10.1179/007817287790176000

9 Colls R (1987) Primitive Methodists in the northern coalfield. In J Obelkevich, L Roper, and R Samul (eds.), *Disciplines of Faith. Studies in Religion, Politics and Patriarchy*. London: Routledge & Kegan Paul; Wearmouth R (1957) *The Social and Political Influence of Methodism in the Twentieth Century*. London: Epworth, ch. 7.

10 Bruce S (2011) Methodism and mining in County Durham, 1881–1991. *Northern History*, 48(2): 337–355. https://doi.org/10.1179/007817211X13061632130674

11 Cooter R (2005) *When Paddy Met Geordie. The Irish in County Durham and Newcastle, 1840–1880*. Sunderland: Sunderland University Press; Neal F (1993) English–Irish conflict in North East England. In P Buckland and J Belchem (eds.), *The Irish in British Labour History*, pp. 59–85. Liverpool: Institute of Irish Studies.

12 Lenders J (1930) *History of the Parish of Sacriston*. Bruges: Gruuthuuse, at 11.

13 Lenders (1930), at 18, see Reference 12.

14 Lenders (1930), at 18, see Reference 12.

15 Lenders (1930), at 70, see Reference 12.

16 Lenders (1930), at 29, see Reference 12.

17 Lenders (1930), at 38, see Reference 12.

18 *Durham Chronicle*, 15 June 1894.

19 Lenders (1930), at 18, see Reference 12.

20 Keating J (1917) The Tyneside Irish Brigade. In F Lavery (ed.), *Irish Heroes in the Great War*. London: Everett & Co.

21 For instance, *Chester-le-Street Chronicle and District Advertiser*, 25 December 1914.

22 Lenders (1930), at 81, see Reference 12.

23 Shannon S (2013) Irish Nationalist Organisations in the North East of England, 1890–1925. Doctoral thesis, Northumbria University, at 163. https://nrl.northumbria.ac.uk/id/eprint/16050/

24 Ross T and Stoddart A (1921) *Jubilee History of Annfield Plan Industrial Cooperative Society Ltd, 1870–1920*. Manchester: Co-operative Wholesale Printing Works.

25 Lamb J and Warren S (1990) *The People's Store. A Guide to the North Eastern Co-op's Family Tree*. Gateshead: North Eastern Co-operative Society.

26 Cole G D H (1944) *A Century of Cooperation*. Manchester: Cooperative Union.

27 *The Builder*, 4 March 1897, 72(2826), at 323–324.

28 Ross and Stoddard (1921), at 67, see Reference 24.

29 Lenders (1930), at 80, see Reference 12.

30 McCullough Thew L (1985) *The Pit Village and the Store. The Portrait of a Mining Past*. London: Pluto, at 71.

31 Oxley J (1924) *The Birth of a Movement. A Tribute the Memory of Joseph Hopper*. Gateshead: Gateshead District Aged Mineworkers Homes; House of Commons (1899) *Second Special Report and Report from the Select Committee on The Cottage Homes Bill, Together with The Proceedings of the Committee, Minutes of Evidence, and Appendix*. Ordered, by The House of Commons, to be Printed, 7 July. London: HMSO, Evidence of Joseph Hopper, pp 117–124; Durham Aged Mineworkers' Homes Association (1909) *An Appreciation of the Life of Joseph Hopper. Pioneer of the Durham Aged Mineworkers' Homes Association*. Durham.

32 Wearmouth (1957), at 134–135, see Reference 9.

33 Major advances in public health were made in County Durham during this period under the leadership of Dr Eustace Hill, Medical Officer of Health. His obituary notes:

Durham, when Eustace Hill went there, was one of the most backward areas in England from a public health standpoint; he left it one of the most progressive.Typhoid and other former scourges were virtually stamped out during his reign at the Shire Hall. The infant mortality rate, which had been something like 300 per 1,000 births, fell to 73. Overcrowding and dreadful housing conditions were ameliorated. A network of health services extended from the Tyne to the Tees.

His obituarist further notes:

Hill's instinctive social sympathies in a densely populated industrial area like Durham gave him an understanding of Labour ideals, and he was proud to serve one of the two county councils—the other being Glamorgan—where Labour was in power.

'Obituary: Sir Eustace Hill', *British Medical Journal* (12 December 1931): 1115–1116. https://doi.org/10.1136/bmj.2.3701.1115

34 Ryder R (1984) Council housebuilding in County Durham, 1900–1938: The local implementation of national policy. In M J Daunton (ed.), *Councillors and Tenants* pp. 39–100. Leicester: Leicester University Press.

35 Tomaney J (2018) The lost world of Peter Lee. *Renewal: A Journal of Social Democracy*, 26(1): 78–82. https://journals.lwbooks.co.uk/renewal/vol-26-issue-1/article-8936/

36 Mattinson D (2020) *Beyond the Red Wall: Why Labour Lost, How the Conservatives Won and What Will Happen Next?* London: Biteback.

37 For instance, Llewelyn Davies M (1931) *Life as We Have Known It. The Voices of Working-Class Women*. London: Hogarth.

38 For a fuller account of this history, see Tomaney J (Forthcoming 2022) Mrs Ann Errington of Sacriston: the political biography of a Durham miner's wife between the wars. *Women's History Review*. https://doi.org/10.1080/09612025.2023.2272102

39 Tomaney (2020), see Reference 7.

6. Root shock: unmaking social infrastructure in Sacriston

Keywords: Sacriston; root shock; social infrastructure; loss

In the previous chapter we described the explosive episode of social infrastructure-making that occurred in Sacriston at end of the 19th and beginning of the 20th centuries. This building frenzy was financed largely from the resources of the village itself—the "pennies and sixpences" of local people—but also, at times, with contributions of land, mainly from the colliery owners. This endowed Sacriston with a wide range of social infrastructure, much of which lasted long into the second half of the 20th century and some of which survives today. Overall, though, there is much reduced provision of social infrastructure in Sacriston today. We chart the long transformation in social infrastructure that began with signs of atrophy in the 1960s, but accelerated in the aftermath of the pit closure and, later, during the decade of austerity. Our story shows that the fate of social infrastructure was affected by public policies over the long run, broader social and economic changes (e.g., rising living standards, secularisation, rising female participation in the workforce, etc.), as well as more recent austerity. In his novel the *Sun Also Rises* (1926), Ernest Hemingway has two of his characters discuss how one of them went bankrupt:

> "How did you go bankrupt?" Bill asked.
>
> "Two ways," Mike said. "Gradually and then suddenly."[1]

In many respects, this formulation captures the decline of social infrastructure in Sacriston.

The year 1945 was a watershed for Sacriston. The newly elected Labour government legislated a major transformation of British society. Notably, key industries were nationalised, that is, taken into state ownership. The most consequential of these nationalisations, for Sacriston, was that of coal. In 1947, the National Coal Board (NCB) replaced the many companies that previously mined Britain's reserves of coal, including the Charlaw and Sacriston Colliery Company Ltd. Nationalisation was a response to the failure of private ownership to modernise the industry. It secured the industry which still supplied the country with fuel and safeguarded work for the men of Sacriston. Whereas Col. Blackett, managing director of the Charlaw and Sacriston Colliery Company from 1890 to 1935, had lived in the village, and his deputy T. F. Brass had been a Methodist minister at the local chapel, the NCB, an agency of national government, was headquartered in London. This signalled a loss of local economic control in the longer run. Indeed, eventually, the NCB became a mechanism for the closure of the industry. Also, the 1945 Labour government enacted a range of social reforms including the extension of pensions and social security rights, the expansion of school education, and the creation of the National Health Service (NHS). All these contributed to improving working-class living standards. But this also meant that assets, infrastructure and services that had once been locally owned or controlled were now under the authority of the national government, reinforcing the position of North East England as a "state managed region".[2] Later, much of this infrastructure and services was privatised.

https://doi.org/10.1080/2578711X.2023.2255001

As Ramsden notes, in the post-war period especially, sociologists and historian posited that "modernity progressively undermined local social ties and attachment to place".[3] Full employment, "affluence" and increased social mobility encouraged "privatism" in working-class life which was increasingly centred on the home. But as Ramsden's own work shows, this is, at best, a partial account of local working-class life after the Second World War. He shows the town of Beverley in East Yorkshire retained a strong sense of place during this period and working-class forms of sociability were transformed rather than erased: "cultures of neighbourhood mutual assistance and gender-divided sociability changed only slowly".[4] This is also true of Sacriston. In part, this reflected the stability of industrial employment during this period, but, as we show below, it also involved the reworking of social infrastructure.

During the 1940s, 1950s and for much of the 1960s, full employment and rising living standards operated alongside an adapted form of traditional sociability. For instance, Sacriston Workmen's Club arguably had its heyday not in the period before the Second World War, but during the 1960s:

> By far, the best era must have been the late 50s, to early 70s when entertainment in the Club was Mondays and Fridays "Disco", Thursday and Saturday "Dancing" and top shows on Sundays and Tuesdays which was known as Steward's Night, when most Stewards took their day off and came to Sacriston from all over the County to meet up with their friends for a night of entertainment and spend a small fortune, it was really a sight to see them returning from the bar with a sea of "shorts" covering the whole of the trays, all were good spenders.[5]

The club continued to play a traditional role in the community, raising money for the families of miners who lost their lives in pit accidents or the Korean War. But now the club attracted nationally recognised entertainers and, significantly, increasing numbers of women were now among the patrons, although not members of the managing committee.[6] Existing social infrastructure was being adapted to changing social circumstances. Institutions such as Sacriston Colliery Cricket Club had a large membership and village sporting fixtures attracted big crowds.[7] Tens of thousands of people attended the Durham Miner's Gala each summer, which was an occasion for the Sacriston Lodge to parade its banner (Figure 6.1).

In the 1950s–70s Sacriston was a thriving place. Economic and community vitality were inextricably linked; most people were far from wealthy, but fulltime work for men was plentiful, wages were rising, work—particularly part-time work—was increasingly available for women, and young families were moving from substandard colliery housing into new, modern council and owner-occupied homes. A strong local economy underpinned a strong community. Families still tended to spend their money and their leisure time mainly in the community where they lived. There were two cinemas in the village. For men in Sacriston, the working

Figure 6.1 1#People of Sacriston with the Lodge banner, Durham Miners' Gala, 1958

Source: Beamish Museum, NEG 73231

men's club and the Catholic Club. There was a dance hall, a bowling green, a library, cinemas and several pubs: "The Robin Hood, George & Dragon, Colliery Inn, The Queen's Head, The Three Horse Shoes" (Hugh, Sacriston Parish Council). Shopping in the Front Street and calls on neighbours afforded opportunities for women to socialise. The village was characterised by a high level of conviviality: "Everybody knew everybody, you knew who lived here and there" (Derek, Parish Council, Fulforth Community Centre). A rich endowment of social infrastructure supported a wide range of sociality.

> So, we had all of these social spaces but then we also had lots of activities going on. We had the Brownies and Guides, the Salvation Army, the church hall, Fyndoune [the local secondary school]. We had a thriving Cubs and Scouts group. … So lots of things to do, regular jumble sales, coffee mornings, fairs, Christmas fairs, Christmas Carol services, all that sort of thing.
>
> (Heather Liddle, Sacriston Enterprise Workshops/Sacriston Youth Group)

Sacriston was spared the problems of Category D villages, described in chapter 4, and in some respects was protected by its Category A status. For instance, Chester-le-Street District Council opened a swimming pool in the village in the 1970s. But the closure of the pool in 2000 caused local resentments. The decision of the council to place a public artwork in the village seemed to rub salt into the wound. Margaret Webster, organiser of the campaign to save the swimming pool, said:

> These plans are an absolute disgrace. Whatever they build with this money, it will be vandalised. What are they going to do anyway—give us Chester-le-Street's answer to the Angel of the North? There is no real point to a work of art in the town—not when they are closing down facilities that are vital to the community.[8]

Despite appearances of stability, changes were afoot. While some social infrastructure, such as the club, was reinvented, other structures began to atrophy. The fate of the Co-op reveals this. In 1948, County Durham had the second highest rate Co-op membership in England and Wales (behind Northamptonshire) and the second highest sales per head.[9] But a decade or so later the Co-op movement in County Durham was struggling.

> Serious problems began to emerge in the 1960s when the run-down started of the North East's traditional industries such as mining, shipbuilding and steel. Inevitably the locally based Societies were badly affected by the resultant withdrawals of share capital, people moving away to find work, and the general reshaping of communities.[10]

The Annfield Plain Industrial Cooperative Society declared record profits in 1960, but, by 1971, the Sacriston branch had closed. The arrival of supermarkets in nearby towns, offering cheaper products, and changing patterns of consumption played a part in its demise. The Annfield Plain Society was forced into a merger and became part of the larger Dunelm Society in 1969, which in turn was absorbed into the North Eastern Co-op in 1990, which itself was absorbed into the national Cooperative Group in 2004. Following the closure of the Sacriston branch, the building was used for a variety of purposes over the years, but eventually ended up derelict and empty.

The deconsecration of St Peter's Anglican church in 2004 reflected another social trend: the secularisation of life. A busy religious life had been a marker of Sacriston at the turn of the 20th century. St Peter's had been built in 1866 and was the centre of religious and social activity for members of the Church of England. The various Methodist sects unified in 1932, eliminating the need for several chapels. Church attendances remained comparatively high until after the Second World War. By the end the of the century they were falling rapidly. The Catholic parish of St Bede's merged with the neighbouring one of St Cuthbert's in Chester-le-Street. The closure of St Peter's, though, left empty a major building on the village Front Street. Efforts to repurpose it failed.[11] A sense of decline pervades accounts of this period.

> There's been an absolutely massive change. We've had so many community buildings, so we had the catholic club, which, although it had a licensed bar, when I was younger there was a youth club there, discos, kids parties. Next to that … there was a communal hall and that would do meals on wheels … at 6 o'clock you'd see the same people passing your house because they were going to the bingo. We had the old community centre, which was huge, absolutely huge.

> And you'd have the playgroup running from there, it had a lunch, a Saturday morning coffee morning ... a toy library, a gym out the back, an office, a function room upstairs with a bar, a lot of meeting rooms ... but wasn't very accessible and it was run down and cheaper to build a new one. The cricket club ... that's more used now as a community space than it's ever been and I think that's because we've lost a lot of the other ones ... we had Graham Court which was sheltered housing and that had a communal room ... the Salvation Army ... and the Methodist Church. The Salvation Army to survive have to let out the rooms. ... But again, it also means that it's getting more community use, whether it's charged or not ... the Working Men's club now gets you a lot of meetings in the rooms, but it's not accessible ....
>
> (Heather Liddle, Sacriston Enterprise Workshops/Sacriston Youth Group)

Even before the closure of the pit, the increase in car use was transforming the spatial patterns of everyday life, making Sacriston Front Street much less of a community space. People increasingly travelled outside the village to shop and for their leisure. This trend accelerated with the growth of retail parks with free parking located on the edge of nearby Durham city. The dense network of connections made on a daily and weekly basis in the streets, by women in the local shops, and by men in the local pubs and clubs was now gone, and many people feel its loss. Women have more options, but also face more pressures. With the decline of male-only social spaces, and the rise of more family-centred leisure activities, men may be more deeply involved in family life, but work for many is defined by precarity and low wages. Higher levels of inequality within the village cause tensions. While often accepting of the inevitability of change, older villagers recall what they regard as valuable from that time—a vibrant local economy, with "rooted" local firms that do more than just sell goods and services, supported by local people earning decent wages and with time, too, to spend in their local economy and community. Moreover, successive waves of local government reform centralised decision-making, rendering political power more remote and inaccessible.

The closure of the pit, however, was the watershed that transformed conditions in the village:

> There was a lot of money in the village when the pit was open, shops were thriving, I mean it was good. I can remember the old co-op and thankfully that's been revived. With the pits closing it sort of dragged the village down. I would personally like to see the Front Street a lot livelier ... the village suffered; the shops suffered. You know the new superstores have affected all the general stores in the village and changed the whole aspect. Even the pubs ... they've all closed.
>
> (Keith Allen, Sacriston Colliery Cricket Club)

Some parts of the village are plagued by antisocial and disorderly behaviour.[12] But, on the fringes, especially in the last decade, new owner-occupied housing has been built in the village, which has further transformed its character. The new private housing has brought a different type of community dynamic:

> A change I have seen is people moving into the village who don't actively socialise ... some people do engage a bit but we know how much the village has changed in the last ten or fifteen years. A lot of people you can see just drive out to go to work, drive back in.
>
> (Keith Allen, Sacriston Colliery Cricket Club)

The relationship of the newcomers to the existing social infrastructure is different to longer standing residents:

> what these people do is, they go to Tesco for a pint of milk on their way home. They don't go to the library. They don't go to the independent shops because they don't have that connection, that's the divide.
>
> (Gemma O'Brien, Sacriston Youth Group)

Overall, social conditions in the village are more social and spatially segregated than when the pit was main provider of (male) jobs, even if, in some respects, gender segregation has reduced.

Austerity accelerated the decline of social infrastructure. Two episodes exemplify the point. The first is the closure of the Sure Start Centre in the village. Sure Start, a UK government programme established in 1998, aimed "to raise the physical, social, emotional and intellectual status of young children through improved services ... targeted at children under four and their families in areas of need".[13] A Sure Start Centre was opened in Sacriston in 2010, with "a cookery demonstration, messy play and a children's entertainer".[14] Several evaluations identified a range of benefits of the Sure Start scheme for children, mothers and families,[15] but hundreds of Sure Start centres were closed as a direct result of austerity measures in the mid-2010s with likely negative impacts on communities.[16] By 2015, faced with the requirement to making swingeing cuts in its expenditure as a result of the reduction in central government funding, Durham County Council proposed to significantly reduce the number of Sure Start Centres across the county and Sacriston was slated for closure.[17] This amounted to the loss of a popular and well-used service that was located at Fyndoune School, which itself was soon closed. Some of the remaking of social infrastructure that we report in the next chapter can be seen as an effort on the part of local people to replace facilities such as the Sure Start Centre which were victims of austerity.

In April 2021, Durham County Council announced the closure of Fyndoune Community College, the secondary school in the village—described as a "merger" with a school in the village of Ushaw Moor, 8 km away.[18] Fyndoune school had experienced falling enrolments and had been designated as "requiring improvement" by the Office for Standards in Education, Children's Services and Skills, a national regulatory agency, although standards were rising at the time it was closed. Durham County Council was under pressure to reduce the costs of secondary education. There had been long-term concerns about the future of the school—which affected enrolments—but local people opposed the closure.[19]

> They closed the school down, saying that it was run down and not enough kids going, but at the same time the County Council announced in the county plan that 400 new homes were going to be built in Sacriston. So now all of our kids have to travel to DCBC [Durham Community Business College] in Bearpark, or Chester-le-Street or Framwellgate Moor, and it's really annoying that our kids are sitting on buses, wheeled in and out.(Derek, Sacriston Parish Council/Fulforth Centre)

The effects of the closure were seen locally as undermining the cohesion and vitality of the community with knock-on effects on other activities. For instance, Sacriston Colliery Cricket Club had run "taster sessions" at the school from which it had recruited junior members. For the cricket club the loss of the school closed a vital recruitment channel.

Klinenberg identifies the importance of social infrastructures used by young people, although their perspectives and unique experiences are rarely considered in these debates. Schools, for instance, are discussed primarily in terms of educational quality and individual student achievement, but they are also places where democratic ideas are established and civic skills learned. In the case of Sacriston, the closure of the local secondary school was experienced as a grievous blow by the local community. Students must now travel to a school in Durham City. Using focus group methods, we found young people from Sacriston have a strong awareness of the strengths and weaknesses of village social infrastructure and have a critical awareness of past and present place identities. Even during their lifetimes, they sense a decline in the quality of social infrastructure and are aware—and supportive—of rebuilding efforts.

We showed in chapter 5 that at the turn of the 20th century Sacriston was furnished with a range of social infrastructure that supported a variety of community activity. By the beginning of the 21st century, though, much of the social infrastructure was denuded. In this chapter, we have charted the unmaking of social infrastructure in Sacriston. Although Sacriston avoided the fate of Category D villages, which were purposely run down, we showed that this unmaking was a long, uneven process, but can be traced back as far as the 1960s. Many factors explain the long-run processes, including industrial restructuring, broader social changes such as secularisation, and the changing role of women in the labour market and in society. The closure of the colliery in 1985 represented a watershed which accelerated decline, while austerity intensified this. The features of "root shock" increasingly were visible. But accelerating decline of social infrastructure also stimulated some in the community to begin the arduous and uncertain process of remaking social infrastructure. We describe these efforts in chapter 7.

NOTES

1 Hemingway E (1926) *The Sun Also Rises*. New York, NY: Charles Scribner's Sons, ch. 13. https://www.gutenberg.org/files/67138/67138-h/67138-h.htm

2 Hudson R (1989) *Wrecking a Region: State Policies, Party Politics and Regional Change in North East England*. London: Pion.

3 Ramsden S (2015) Remaking working-class community: Sociability, belonging and "affluence" in a small town, 1930–80. *Contemporary British History*, 29(1): 1–26. https://doi.org/10.1080/13619462.2014.951338

4 Ramsden (2015), at 9, see Reference 3.

5 Rand D and Claughan L (2002) *Sacriston Workmen's Club, 1902–2002*. Chester-le-Street: privately published, at 17.

6 Among the entertainers who appeared at Sacriston at this time were The Walker Brothers and Marty Wilde. Larger working men's clubs in the wider region were capable of attracting The Beatles and The Rolling Stones. This was the golden age of working men's clubs with a growing presence of women among audiences.

7 Chapman J (2002) *Cream Teas and Nutty Slack. A History of Club Cricket in County Durham, 1751–2002*. Chester-le-Street: privately published.

8 *Northern Echo* (2000) Pool campaigners criticise art scheme. *Northern Echo*, 30 August. https://www.thenorthernecho.co.uk/news/7131667.pool-campaigners-criticise-art-scheme/

9 Cole G D H (1951) *The British Co-operative Movement in Socialist Society*. London: Routledge & Kegan Paul.

10 Lamb J and Warre S (1990) *The People's Store. A Guide to the North Eastern Co-op's Family Tree*. Gateshead: North Eastern Co-operative.

11 *Northern Echo* (2013) Former church now ready for use. *Northern Echo*, 6 May. https://www.thenorthernecho.co.uk/news/10402078.former-church-now-ready-community-use/

12 *Northern Echo* (2021) Closure order on Sacriston house which plagued community. *Northern Echo*, 15 December. https://www.thenorthernecho.co.uk/news/19785719.closure-order-sacriston-house-plagued-community/

13 Glass N (1999) Sure Start: The development of an early intervention programme for young children in the United Kingdom. *Children and Society*, 13(4): 257–264. https://doi.org/10.1002/CHI569

14 *Northern Echo* (2010) Children's centre opened. *Northern Echo*, 23 February. https://www.thenorthernecho.co.uk/news/local/northdurham/5024094.childrens-centre-opened/

15 Cattan S et al. (2021) *The Health Impacts of Sure Start* (Briefing Note BN332). London: Institute of Fiscal Studies (IFS). https://ifs.org.uk/uploads/BN332-The-health-impacts-of-sure-start-1.pdf; Sammons P et al. (2015) *The Impact of Children's Centres: Studying the Effects of Children's Centres in Promoting Better Outcomes for Young Children and Their Families Evaluation of Children's Centres in England*. Oxford: Oxford University. https://assets.publishing.service.gov.uk/government/uploads/system/uploads/attachment_data/file/485347/DFE-RB495_Evaluation_of_children_s_centres_in_England__the_impact_of_children_s_centres_brief.pdf

16 Torjesen I (2016) Austerity cuts are eroding benefits of sure start children's centres. *British Medical Journal*, 352: i335. https://doi.org/10.1136/bmj.i335

17 Durham County Council (2015) *Cabinet. Review of Children's Centres in County Durham. Key Decision: CAS/10/13. Report of Corporate Management Team.* 18 March. https://democracy.durham.gov.uk/documents/s49646/Childrens%20Centre%20Review%20FINAL.pdf

18 Durham County Council (2021) *Cabinet. Proposal to Amalgamate Durham Community Business College and Fyndoune Community College into a Single Secondary School on the site of Durham Community Business College. Key Decision: CYPS/01/2021. Report of Cabinet of Corporate Management Team*, 12 April. https://democracy.durham.gov.uk/documents/s131918/Proposal%20to%20close%20Fyndoune.pdf

19 *Northern Echo* (2018) School community unites against proposed Durham Federation changes. *Northern Echo*, 23 June. https://www.thenorthernecho.co.uk/news/16308175.school-community-unites-proposed-durham-federation-changes/

7. Radical hope: remaking social infrastructure in Sacriston

Keywords: Sacriston; radical hope; social infrastructure; place attachments

In chapter 5 we charted the long and uneven process of social infrastructure-making in Sacriston from 1850, which endowed the village with a range of facilities that supported communal activities. We also showed how the crucial component of this era of social infrastructure-making was the "pennies and sixpences" of miners and their families, but we also acknowledged the contributions of the coal company. This collective enterprise gave expression to Sacriston as a moral community. In chapter 6, we chronicled the unmaking of social infrastructure from the 1960s. Again, this was a long and uneven process. In key respects, avoiding the fate of Category D villages elsewhere in County Durham, the 1950s and 1960s represented a high point for the village. It was the heyday of the Working Men's Club but, by the end of the decade, the Co-op, opened with such fanfare in 1897, had closed, signalling bigger problems ahead. The rundown of social infrastructure accelerated after the closure of the pit and during the decade of austerity, but we set this decline in the context of longer term and broader social and economic change. Current social infrastructure is shown in Figure 7.1.

In recent years, though, Sacriston has witnessed a new episode of social infrastructure-making, perhaps not on the scale of a century or more ago, but highly significant, nevertheless. In this chapter, we describe and account for this remaking of social infrastructure. At its heart lies the effort of a relatively small number of highly committed and entrepreneurial local people who have identified unmet needs and sought to address them, despite unpropitious circumstances, by building or repurposing social infrastructure. Whereas the early social infrastructure building in the village depended on the "pennies and sixpences" of miners and their families, recent efforts rely more on external resources, which poses challenges. But local social entrepreneurs have proved adept at attracting investment and somehow managing to survive. These interventions represent "radical hope", in the terms we discussed in chapter 3, in an effort to act and think anew as an old world passes. This is a largely untold and, certainly, unheralded story that echoes the very final observation made by George Eliot in her novel *Middlemarch* (1871–72), that:

> the growing good of the world is partly dependent on unhistoric acts; and that things are not so ill with you and me as they might have been, is half owing to the number who lived faithfully a hidden life, and rest in unvisited tombs.[1]

The Sacriston story, simultaneously ordinary and epic, sheds light on the conditions under which social infrastructure is made in a "left behind" place, revealing both the promise and the challenge. We show that the social infrastructure (re)makers draw upon a strong sense of local attachment, an awareness of the distinctive history of the village, but adapt these resources to meet new challenges. In this chapter we focus on two important episodes in the remaking of social infrastructure: the creation of the Fulforth Centre, which was replaced by Memorial Hall in the village, and the rebirth of the Co-op building.

https://doi.org/10.1080/2578711X.2023.2255003

Figure 7.1 Social infrastructure in Sacriston, County Durham, 2022

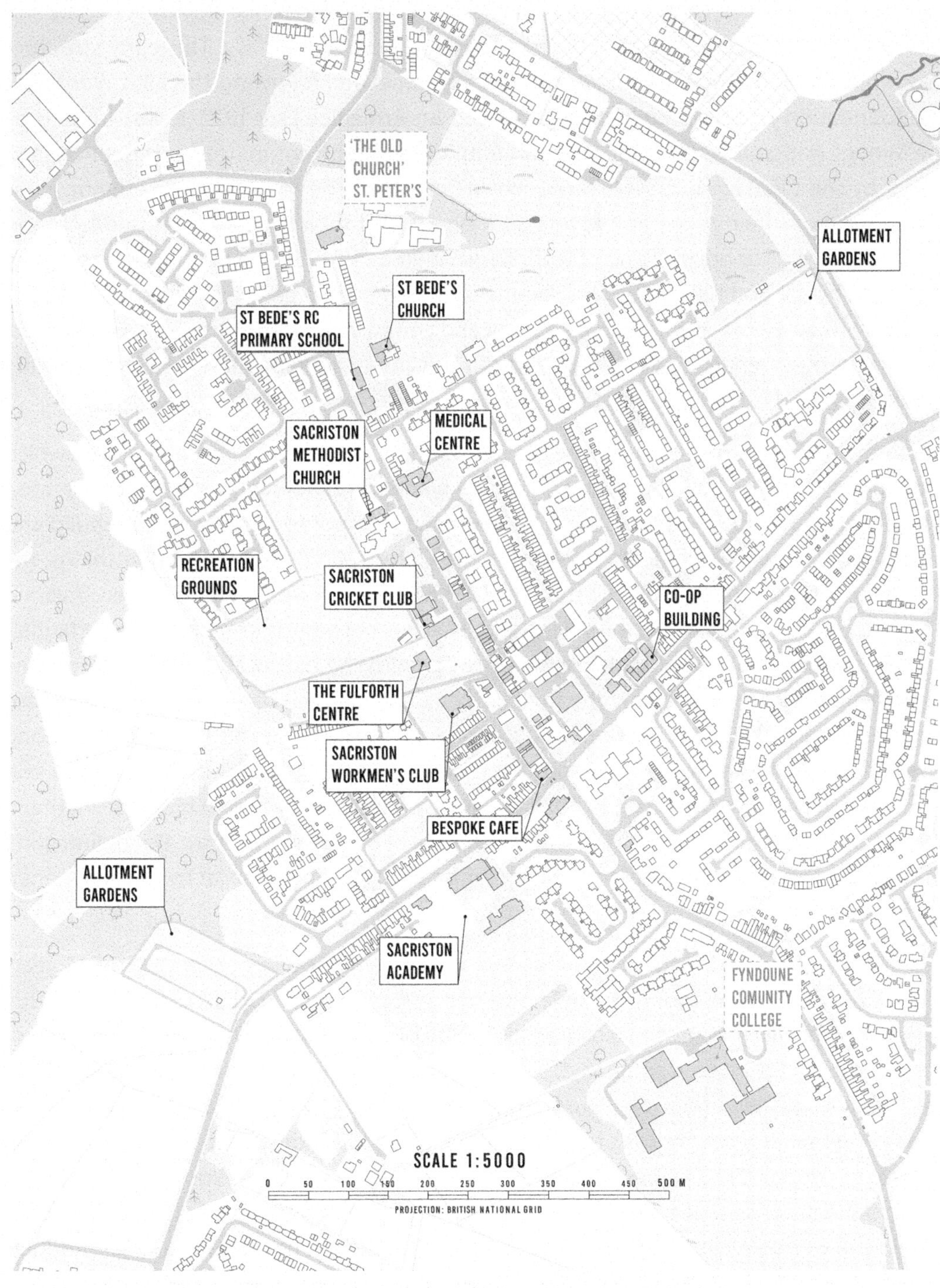

Sources: Digimap Ordnance Survey, https://digimap.edina.ac.uk/os (accessed on 28 September 2021); adapted by the authors
Note: Scale 1:5000

The Literary Institute appears on early maps of Sacriston. It was supported by subscriptions from miners, but business directories suggest it was also funded by the Charlaw and Sacriston Colliery Company. It included a reading room and library. This early structure was replaced by the Memorial Institute, on the same site, following the First Word War. The foundation stone of the Institute was laid on Armistice Day 1922. It was funded by the Miners' National Welfare Fund, a joint employers–union committee and built on land gifted by the Charlaw and Sacriston Colliery Company. The stone-laying ceremony was a major village affair which employers and miners and their families attended.[2] Among other things, it once housed one of the village cinemas. In 1961, the building was severely damaged by fire and hastily rebuilt. The Institute had been a centre of village activity for generations and a place where many family and community occasions had been marked, but was in poor repair by the 1990s and did not meet modern safety and accessibility requirements.

Proposals for the future of the Institute proved contentious because of the affection in which the old building was held. Some in the village wanted the building modernised because it symbolised a historic identity, but it was deemed cheaper to demolish and rebuild and it was replaced by a new building known as the Fulforth Centre. Among other things, the centre contains the roll of war dead from the First and Second World Wars. The new building occupies a prominent place in the village and itself has become a centre for social activities. A small square built in front of the new centre contains the part of the pit wheel from the colliery and coal tub and is now the location for activities such the annual Remembrance Day observances (Figure 7.2).[3] The struggle to raise the funds for this purpose was a long one with original plans scaled back, but the centre is now the base for the activities of several village groups. For instance, in 2022, a well-attended celebration to mark the Platinum Jubilee of the reign of Queen Elizabeth II took place at the Fulforth Centre. But maintaining the building results in a constant struggle to raise funds and find new activities that generate income.

Second, the Co-op building, opened in 1897, which had stood largely empty for 15 years before 2019, also after a long struggle, was repurposed and brought back into use. One early problem was that the legal ownership of the building was unclear for some time. But a new "community interest company", Sacriston Enterprise Workshops, was established and the building was leased to it by Durham County Council in 2019, for a nominal payment. The Co-op building now houses four independent organisations, although there is a high degree of cooperation between them and plans to attract others. Woodshed Workshop is a social enterprise that trains young people, who are not in education, employment or training, in woodworking skills. It designs and creates wooden furniture and other products through the use of reclaimed, recycled, reused, and ethically and locally sourced wood. The young people trained at Woodshed typically are highly vulnerable and have fallen out

Figure 7.2 Winding wheel memorialising Sacriston Colliery outside the Fulforth Centre

Source: Carl Watson (with permission)
Note: The text on the pavement names the coal seams worked at the pit: Victoria, Brockwell, Hutton, Brass Thill, Low Main, Main Coal and Five-Quarter

of the school system. Recycld runs a shop that sells reclaimed wood products. Sacriston Youth Project provides out-of-school activities for children and young people who would not otherwise have access to them. Live Well North East provides a range of health-related activities and runs a boxing gym. The Co-op building is now a hive of activity and symbolic of progress in the village: "It's the sense of ownership. It's the sense of belonging. The space is yours. And I think that's what works" (Gemma O'Brien, Sacriston Youth Group). Funding these activities is a constant struggle in an era of austerity. Moreover, local authorities are viewed as remote, inflexible and bureaucratic. For instance, when the local secondary school closed, the parish council wanted to develop the site as a home for a local football club, but the plans became mired in bureaucracy. Typically, where support is offered it is for capital projects rather than ongoing running costs. Local actors have become adept at bypassing these obstacles. For instance, Sacriston Youth Project has struck up a relationship with a private foundation that has supported its activities in ways government funders seem unable to.

What accounts for this new wave of social infrastructure-building in Sacriston in conditions that in many ways are hostile? One important aspect of the answer to this question concerns a powerful sense of belonging and deep commitment to place. The chairperson of the Fulforth Centre states categorically, "I run the centre because of a love for Sacriston" (Linda Surtees, Fulforth Centre). Those involved in the provision of social infrastructure make deep and long commitments, "I've been here that long now that at the presentation evening for the seniors, I remembered them when they were titchies [young children]" (Keith Allen, Sacriston Cricket Club).

Sacriston Cricket Club is more than a sporting venue. It is a space for growing up in the village and during the COVID-19 pandemic was involved in the provision of food to the housebound. Place attachments foster commitments and furnish the "local knowledge" that helps identify unmet needs and offer practical solutions to them:

> there's your connection to place and I'll work with people from our area ... and probably tolerate far more than I should actually tolerate because I'm more drawn to the stories of the people I work with, and I get more actively involved because I'm from this place. I really employ from the local pool ... all DH7 [Sacriston postcode], brought up in and around here and that's probably as much training as you need with it! If you have lived experience with this area and you've got different approaches to it, you know.
>
> (Nathan Hopkins, Sacriston Enterprise Workshops/Woodshed)

The various projects underway in the village arise from a desire to meet needs and strengthen the community in a context in which market and state have failed and where traditional forms of politics have been found wanting. So, for instance, although the primary purpose of Sacriston Youth Project is to provide childcare, its role is bigger. Moreover, this role is narrated in terms of the reinvention of the civic and political traditions of the village.

> I think we have a very, very different project to many youth projects because we're not really a youth project, we're a community service disguised as a youth project. So, most youth projects will do from like age 11 to like 16. Whereas we do from like pre-birth to death. Which is the Co-op ethos—cradle to the grave.
>
> (Gemma O'Brien, Sacriston Youth Group)

 https://doi.org/10.1080/2578711X.2023.2255003

This insight has crucial implications for policymakers, who tend to look for quick fixes that can be rolled out centrally rather than engage with actors on the ground who carry the burden of remaking social infrastructure in unpropitious conditions, as we show below.

Deep commitment and reserves of patience are required on the part of the (re)makers of social infrastructure in several respects:

> The kids I work with, they're the worst behaved kids ever in the area. I like every single one of them so don't get us wrong when I say that, but their behaviour is terrible. One of the reasons their behaviour is terrible is because no one will trust them. They know they're not trusted. It's a cycle and you have to break it. I always say "I'm going to trust you" and I get a lot of people saying I'm too soft and I give too many chances but I'll keep on trusting because it's got to stop at some point... eventually you'll balance the scales but it takes a lot of time, money and resource and sometimes it's easier to just lock it away; "no, you're not using that" kind of thing.... We do have examples of the kids not taking the help on board, over and over.... So, what I try to do and sometimes it's really, really frustrating, for all of the staff.... But I would say, what you do is, you plant seeds, you know, so like between the age of 14–24, you just give them little nuggets—"that's not normal". You know, "you shouldn't do that." Plant them and then they'll not come to fruition until you don't know them anymore.... These are the things that you saw in the past start growing. But it's a real problem if you are trying to get funding as its unquantifiable.
>
> (Nathan Hopkins, Sacriston Enterprise Workshops/Woodshed Workshop)

Making these commitments does rest on a carefully calculated cost–benefit ratio but rather on "leaps of faith" and acts of care, albeit based on deep local attachments and knowledge, aimed at addressing local needs.

The (re)makers of social infrastructure face the challenge of engaging with officialdom and bureaucracies. The repurposing of the Co-op building was fraught with difficulty.

> Working with the local authority was a nightmare. Absolute nightmare. Because in County Durham, it's big. And it dominates such a big area.... They didn't know the building belonged to them and the process of unpicking that was so slow.
>
> (Gemma O'Brien, Sacriston Youth Group)

The parish council[4] which, at the time of writing, was championing a sports centre and hub at the now closed Fyndoune school site (see chapter 6), was finding the bureaucratic nature of the county council slow and frustrating:

> From late 2019 we were aware that Durham United Football Club wanted to move up there and take over the fields. We've also worked closely with our MP and the leader of the County Council to see if we [the Parish Council] could take it over and the Football Club lease it on a long-term basis so that could attract funding. But then there were elections, and Labour lost the election!

So, we've started from scratch again. We're now having to wait for Department of Education's Schedule 1 to finish so no one else can take over the school. It's been going on for four years now and it's been very disappointing that people can't tell you the truth.

(Hughie Dixon, Sacriston Parish Council/Fulforth Centre)

Funding crises are perennial. Organising, creating and managing social infrastructure is a hand-to-mouth, month-to-month activity. Funding sources are opaque, difficult to access and uncertain, and there is competition for them. Endless rounds of bidding for resources, even if successful, absorb time that could be allocated to more productive uses and, at times, saps the morale of the best and most resilient of people. Typically, where support is offered it is for capital projects, but revenue support for ongoing running costs is more difficult to obtain. Reporting requirements are onerous for small organisations. At the same time, local actors have become adept are working in these complex systems.

Funding wise it's difficult, we're all competing against each other, all of us here providing all this and we're linked so it's strange, to have to compete for funding. You know, we got funding last year because we don't want to have to charge kids to come and play and put pressure on people to pay money.

(Keith Allen, Sacriston Cricket Club)

There's kind of two models of work in Sacriston Enterprise Workshops because there's some stuff that gets really well funded like the sports bit ... so the Live Well centre, the Government will just chuck money at sports, kick a football and they'll give you a ten grand ... they've got a huge pot of money. Sacriston Youth Group, they've got a pot of funding. ... Us, even though we do get some funding in, it's more of a difficult, complex mix. Our existence at Woodshed is a bit more precarious because it is far more complex.

(Nathan Hopkins, Sacriston Enterprise Workshops/Woodshed Workshops)

Despite the achievements of the new generation of social infrastructure builders a pall of uncertainty lies over these activities and the lack of longer term resources and requirements of funders limits what can be achieved locally.

For Woodshed, our strengths are we all come from this lived experience, we've got like, really deep, deep rooted sort of benefits to the people we work with, but we work with such small numbers and that could be a weakness in its own right. But we're in constant threat of closure, you know, constantly. In the back of my head, I never plan more than six months ahead. I do in terms of business, I've got all these like grand but it can go South very quickly because we're juggling complex issues and complex funding. And you know, I'm not a project coordinator, I'm not like coming from that background, but I know that I'm not a businessman, anything like that. You know, I'm a woodworker who does good stuff with kids. ... We're getting in people to do his English and Maths. ... For the first time ever he's actually engaged with a tutor ... for the first time

> he ever met her, you know, he said fuck this … she went away for a week and I had to do a bit of coaching around it in, you know, do this blah blah blah and the next time she comes and he does the worksheets. And, you know, that's a massive step. But like, I can't even begin to record that and give it to the education provider because they'll not see it as enough. Same with funders.
>
> (Nathan Hopkins, Sacriston Enterprise Workshops/Woodshed Workshops)

However, the fact that the Woodshed was a social enterprise is a helpful way to counteract issues with funding:

> Funders, the big funders, they just want data, data, numbers, numbers, numbers … that actually cuts us off a bit from those kinds of funders because I'm not going to work with a couple hundred people … I can't do it, I work in a very concentrated way. You can't say [to funders], I'll work with five kids a year and change their lives, it's not enough. So that's why we're a social enterprise, the idea is we create stuff and sell it, we're not for profit.
>
> (Nathan Hopkins, Sacriston Enterprise Workshops/Woodshed Workshops)

Local actors have become adept at bypassing these obstacles. But there are great risks if this relationship is lost. There is a strong articulated desire to move away from competitive, distracting and exhausting funding cycles and a more collaborative and sustainable approach in both Sacriston and other villages.

The revitalised Co-op building contains valuable social infrastructure that meets needs within the village. But its revitalisation serves another purpose: bringing back to life a prominent building in the centre for the village, which is welcomed by residents. The Co-op is now a place people drop into when passing by, rather than a derelict building they hurry past. In a focus group, schoolchildren, when asked to describe the things they liked in the village, unprompted, mentioned the window displays and lighting in the Co-op building. This provides support for the suggestion in chapter 2 that bringing old buildings back to life brings visible improvements to places and sense that good things are happening.

Improved social infrastructure does not solve all the problems faced by Sacriston, but recent actions to remake social infrastructure in Sacriston bear the strong imprint of "radical hope", in the way described by Jonathan Lear (see chapter 2). Faced with the loss of not just of a key industry but a way of life, the remakers of social infrastructure in Sacriston see their task as creating something new out of resources bequeathed from the past. Strong local attachments are a driving force behind the desire to make improvements in the village. And there is strong sense of history on the part the (re)makers of social infrastructure which inspires current efforts but by providing a foundation for moving forward. In the final chapter, we offer some reflection and policy implications arising from our study of Sacriston.

NOTES

1 Eliot G (1871–72). *Middlemarch, A Study of Provincial Life*, 8 bks. London: William Blackwood & Sons. https://www.gutenberg.org/files/145/145-h/145-h.htm#chap87
2 *Chester-le-Street Chronicle and District Advertiser*, 17 November 1922.
3 The coal tub was donated to the village by Augustine "Gus" Tomaney, to whom this book is dedicated.
4 Parish councils are highly localised elected representative bodies with very minimal powers and resources.

8. Conclusions and policy implications

Keywords: left behind places; social infrastructure; regional policy; levelling up

8.1 FINDINGS

We began this book by noting the growing academic and policy interest in the role of social infrastructure in "left behind places". We set out to develop a deeper understanding of the making, unmaking and remaking of social infrastructure in "left behind" places. Our understanding is derived from a "deep place study" of a former coalmining community of Sacriston in County Durham, north-east England. But our theory, methods and findings have wider applicability. The existing literature on social infrastructure comprises numerous efforts to measure, quantify and tabulate "left behindness", but we have attempted to move beyond an understanding of "left behind places" as artefacts of socio-economic data, which demonstrate how much they lag behind national averages. The use of quantitative data allows us to map the provision of social infrastructure, but runs the risk of presenting a static picture. The provisioning of social infrastructure is a historical process and part of active place-making founded on attachments and belonging. It is this process which we have described and analysed.

We attended, in particular, to the affective dimensions of place and, in chapter 2, offered an understanding of "left behind places" as "moral communities", founded on place attachments. Our understanding of social infrastructure recognises its importance in the built environment of places, but also stresses the social relations these contain and enable. Moral communities are given expression in the making of social infrastructure. The unmaking of social infrastructure is both cause and effect of the emergence of left behind places. Today, "left behind" places exhibit major deficiencies in the provision of social infrastructure. The destruction or devaluation of social infrastructure affect "root shock" that can rupture the collective bonds that anchor us in the places in which we live and have made our commitments. These effects seem stronger in places whose identity rests heavily on a single industry, where redundant jobs and destroyed social infrastructure signal the end of a way of life. Such disruptions are described using the language of bereavement and loss. The term "left behind" is pejorative. It conveys a limiting judgement and risks pathologising places. But "left behind places" are constantly being repaired and reconstructed, primarily by people who choose to remain. Strong local identities and place attachments are assets and resources that are critical in the remaking of social infrastructure. A new generation of social infrastructure-makers in "left behind places" deploys "radical hope" to navigate the challenges of renewal in order to make hope practical rather than despair convincing.

The methods we deployed in this study were described in chapter 3. They allow us to move beyond static accounts of the provisioning of social infrastructure and to add depth to quantitative analyses. We developed an intensive research approach focused on identifying underlying causality in the making, unmaking and remaking of social infrastructure. In order to better understand the affective dimension of "left behindness" and the role of social infrastructure, our research was informed by an "ethnographic sensibility". Sacriston was selected

https://doi.org/10.1080/2578711X.2023.2255004 Regional Studies Policy Impact Books as a "critical case" in which the making and unmaking of social infrastructure was likely to be identified. But we adopted an "extended case" approach that situates the story of the village in its wider social, economic and political context. The framing of this case study was undertaken by a "community of inquirers" to produce useful findings. Within this framework we deployed a set of mixed methods: cartography, archival and oral history, site observation, semi-structured interview and focus groups. Each of these methods has strengths and weaknesses, but considered together they produce a multifaceted and deeper understanding of the historical processes behind the making, unmaking and remaking of social infrastructure and have implications for our discussion of policy below.

We explored these ideas and deployed these methods in Sacriston. Our detailed findings are reported in chapters 6–8. We charted the wave of social infrastructure-making that took place in the second half of the 19th century and the first half of the 20th century that gave expression to a distinctively placed-based "moral community". This took the form of "invented traditions"[1] of cooperation, mutuality and an ethic of care. These local activities were connected to larger social and political action that linked the village to the county, the nation and beyond, but the village maintained a strong identity. At the heart of the village was the pit which provided employment for men. Work at the pit was dangerous and intermittent, but was the foundation of the local economy, and it allowed the accumulation of "pennies and sixpences" from the wages of miners, congregations of chapels and churches, and the variety of clubs and associations that, together with contributions from the colliery company, provide the material basis for the making of this social infrastructure. This was a highly gendered world, dominated by male breadwinners, but women were active makers of social infrastructure and, in some prominent cases, leaders of their moral community.

The election of the Labour government in 1945 was a watershed for this world. Nationalisation of coal and other key industries, together with the creation of the "welfare state", brought national government more directly into the day-to-day life and everyday economy of the village, although these trends were underway in the decades before. This brought some benefits but extended the distance between decision-makers and residents. It took time for the consequences of these changes to become apparent. Full employment, new opportunities for women, rising living standards and well-endowed social infrastructure meant that, although not a wealthy place, the post-war period created halcyon days for Sacriston. It is this period that older residents refer to when they discuss better times. This is often misunderstood as misplaced nostalgia for hard times. In an interview with the *Financial Times*, Hilary Clinton suggested, "Whether they were from West Virginia or Tyneside, their lives were so grim and disease-prone and unhygienic—but the nostalgia for those days. I don't know."[2] But people in Sacriston are not nostalgic for mining disasters, unemployment, emphysema or dysentery. Rather they lament a lost era of relative prosperity based on secure local employment and the erosion of the community bonds that were the basis for their struggle to improve life in the village, which produced genuine "pride in place". It takes more than government funds for hanging baskets, referred to in chapter 1, to address this sense of loss and its consequences.

Signs of a chronic crisis in social infrastructure began to appear just as full employment seemed secure, symbolised by the crisis of the Co-operative movement in the 1960s. From the 1980s, a more pervasive sense of decline through deindustrialisation and the erosion of public services shaped County Durham. The closure of Sacriston Colliery in 1985 and the decade of austerity after 2010 created an acute crisis in the village, providing the conditions for "root shock" as a way of life disappeared.

Loss and decline are an important part of the story, but so too is resilience and a strong sense of community and local identity. There are fresh opportunities for some and the arrival of new people in the village. The resilience of the community was demonstrated during the COVID-19 pandemic when, a local headteacher told us, the hard-wiring of a mining community kicked in to provide a communal response to the crisis, of a type which she saw lacking in the middle-class village where she lived, where the response to the crisis was more individualised. This communal response is also evident in local efforts to mitigate and the "cost-of-living-crisis" that emerged in 2022. In recent years, there have been attempts to remake social infrastructure in the village. Small but highly committed groups of residents have restored existing buildings and created new do-it-yourself services that respond to unmet needs in the community. In the absence of "pennies and sixpences" clipped from the proceeds of a productive local economy, efforts to remake social infrastructure rely on external resources—national and local state, philanthropy—but also on the strong and enduring place attachments and a sense of belonging shared by the re-makers. Often at odds with official definitions of problems and solutions, the remaking of social infrastructure is founded on "radical hope" and efforts to overcome despair and make hope practical.

8.2 BEYOND PRIDE IN PLACE

Four major policy implications arise from the analysis presented in this book. They arise from our findings and the methods we deployed. First, we have demonstrated the importance of social infrastructure. There have been efforts to measure the economic contribution, but our data show that as well as contributing to meeting pressing social needs, social infrastructure contributes to a broader sense of community belonging and sense of place which, while difficult to quantify, has many positive local effects. This might not have immediate and conventional economic impacts but contributes significantly to local identity and helps to underpin community well-being. The loss of social infrastructure can similarly have long-term impacts that barely figure in the calculations of policymakers. There is no register of social infrastructure held either nationally or locally, exemplified by the uncertainty surrounding

 https://doi.org/10.1080/2578711X.2023.2255004

the ownership of the Cooperative Buildings before its acquisition by Sacriston Enterprise Workshops, one of the most important historic buildings in the village.

Second, we have shown that the making of social infrastructure is a long-term process. In Sacriston social infrastructure endowments were created over generations, involving intergenerational commitments. This is partly what contributes to the powerful sense of loss—"root shock"—that arises when social infrastructure is diminished or destroyed. Current policy frameworks, especially as they are designed in the UK, around endless competitions for short-term resources—often for capital projects, rather than the revenue support that ensues sustainability—are inimical to creating the conditions for the long-term development of social infrastructure.

Third, we show that social infrastructure is built from the bottom up, expressing local values and needs through community action. This is evident from the Sacriston story, where both the making and remaking of social infrastructure relied on "determined, practical people making things—happen finding work arounds, not taking no for an answer".[3] Thus, the provision of social infrastructure cannot be legislated centrally, although this is the implication of the UK government's Levelling Up White Paper, its various centrally disbursed, competitively allocated funds. It seems to lie behind the belief in the power of hanging baskets. The remaking of social infrastructure relies on the attachments and commitments of local people.

Fourth, the local state has been enfeebled by austerity, but a rebuilt local government will be insufficient and will need to share power with local communities in the field of social infrastructure. The state has a role in enabling the provision social infrastructure and supporting local action but cannot assert its primacy, not least because past experience has fomented distrust about its motives and competences. In the UK, the proposal for a "Community Power Act", including a "community right to buy" assets of local value, and a "community covenant" between state organisations and local people, certainly speak to the experience of Sacriston. But the associated proposal for a national Community Power Commissioner, while welcome, does not go far enough because it misses the crucial importance of the local scale.[4] All local councils should have such a role or equivalent. For instance, the proposed new Mayoral Combined Authority for North East England should consider creating a Community Power Commissioner charged, among things, with developing a strategy for rebuilding social infrastructure.[5]

The Levelling Up White Paper sees "pride in place" as component of what it terms "a contemporary Medici model"[6]—a reference to the conditions that produced the flourishing of Renaissance Florence, including "the magnetic attraction of people, culture, commerce and finance spreading ideas, innovation and ultimately growth".[7] This ambition sounds ridiculous when applied to Sacriston, where needs are basic and pressing and include how to reduce loneliness and isolation, improve health and well-being, and divert young men from involvement with the criminal justice system. Rebuilt social infrastructure is best seen as a component of the foundational (or "everyday") economy—which includes health, care, education, housing, utilities and food supply—because these basic goods and services underpin welfare and citizenship.[8] Moreover, Sacriston does not need a Medici model—as we have shown, it has, to use the language of the White Paper, its own "social narrative" for the making of social infrastructure drawn from its own history that tells of place attachment, moral community, root shock and radical hope. Even within County Durham, Sacriston's story is unique, as we have tried to show. Our methods allow us to reveal that social infrastructure cannot be legislated centrally because it requires the generational commitments of local people. Our methods are policy recommendations—we need deeper understandings of the diverse conditions and motivations that lead to a remaking of social infrastructure in "left behind" places if we stand a chance of achieving long-term and sustainable change. The task of government should not be to define targets and operate policy levers in Whitehall or County Hall, but to enable communities to help themselves by empowering change-makers, building organisational capacity and enabling them by furnishing them with the resources they need to meet the needs in their communities.

8.3 POLICY PROPOSALS

Social infrastructure affords a range of important overlapping, often intangible, benefits, which are difficult to quantify using conventional methods because such methods of value, for example, benefit–cost ratios, are poorly configured to measure it. The (re)makers of social infrastructure respond to perceived local needs rather than calculations of costs and benefits of investments. They are motivated by an ethic of care for their community, draw upon attachments to place and a sense of belonging, and enact shared values. It is hard to put a price on these, but they are the basic nourishment for communities. Conventional investment appraisal approaches favour projects that generate quick and cheap returns in places where growth is strong. This undervalues the contribution of social infrastructure in "left behind places" whose returns are likely to be long term—perhaps generational—but can address problems such as loneliness, which have tangible health impacts that place heavy costs on already burdened medical systems. Public and private systems of investment appraisal need to reflect this. Policymakers should guard against the unmaking of social infrastructure.[9] Its closure in austere times often promises quick solutions to strained public budgets, but the long-term consequences of its loss are now apparent.

The (re)makers of social infrastructure have proved imaginative and adept at overcoming these barriers, but it is easier to obtain finance for capital projects than revenue support. In the long-run revenue support is crucial to success. In the UK, needs-based spending formulae, controlled nationally and targeted at places and projects that meet national criteria, neglect places where spending could be most impactful. Greater resource allocation to local

 https://doi.org/10.1080/2578711X.2023.2255004

government and local discretion in its allocation is a necessary requirement of a strategy for remaking social infrastructure. Competitive bidding processes often pitch local organisations against each other for government funding, duplicate efforts and waste scarce resources that could be better directed to the core objectives of social infrastructure providers.[10]

Often local organisations are working in isolation. There is scope to create networks of social infrastructure providers to share knowledge, experience and build economies of scale and scope. Philanthropy has filled in some of the gaps left by the withdrawal of the state and market, but it can reproduce some of the problems of the state: lack of long-term commitment, the imposition of top-down priorities, lack of transparency and accountability, and faulty valuation of costs and benefits.

Social infrastructure takes a long time to build. It involves long-term commitments to place-making. The (re)making of social infrastructure cannot be legislated centrally but rests on sustained local action. Indeed, centralisation of policymaking is a likely cause of its decline. Devolved structures of government are a necessary but insufficient condition for the (re)making of social infrastructure. Local councils should act as enablers of community action, rather than substitute it. One practical and useful activity that should be undertaken by local and regional governments is to create registers of social infrastructure assets in order to develop better strategies. There are challenges here for university research. How do universities put their knowledge and expertise to work in "left behind places"? How do they empower and enable the (re)makers of social infrastructure?

Recent discussion has tended to link the decline of social infrastructure to the impact of austerity policies—notably in the UK since 2010—but we show that decline has been long-term process in "left behind places", linked to deindustrialisation and associated labour market changes, changing retail, leisure and housing markets, shifting gender relations, etc.—indicating the scale of the challenge in its rebuilding. "Left behindness" itself is often a long-term condition that has its origins well before recent political shocks. Social infrastructure should be seen as a component of the "foundational (or everyday) economy", that is, it concerns the basic requirements of civilised life in all communities, rather than contributing narrowly to "economic growth", "productivity" or "innovation".[11] Social infrastructure supports associational life that is a component of healthy democracies.

Finally, our methods themselves are a key policy recommendation. The sustained immersion entailed in a "deep place" study demonstrates that building social infrastructure long-term commitments that harness the power of belonging and collective memory, and the use of productive nostalgia to instil hope and rekindle potential. Place, neighbourhood, communal cultures, stories and memory need to be rewritten into the politics and policy of social infrastructure because they are integral to the successful (re)making of social infrastructure. We call for a long-term financial commitment to a programme for the rebuilding of social infrastructure in "left behind places" that is led by local communities but enabled by strategic intervention on the part of local, regional and national government, philanthropy and private actors. To yield its wider ranging and longer term benefits, rebuilding social infrastructure should be a central objective of local regeneration plans.

NOTES

1 Hobsbawm E and Ranger T (eds.) (1983) *The Invention of Tradition*. Cambridge: Cambridge University Press.

2 Luce E (2022) Hillary Clinton: "We are standing on the precipice of losing our democracy". *Financial Times*, 17 June. https://www.ft.com/content/2e667c3f-954d-49fa-8024-2c869789e32f

3 We're Right Here (2022) *Introducing the Community Power Act*, p 7. https://www.newlocal.org.uk/publications/introducing-the-community-power-act/

4 We're Right Here (2022), see Reference 3.

5 On the proposed new governance structures for north-east England, see Department for Levelling Up, Housing and Communities (DLUHC) et al. (2022) *North East Devolution Deal*. https://assets.publishing.service.gov.uk/government/uploads/system/uploads/attachment_data/file/1144144/North_East_Devolution_deal.pdf

6 Department for Levelling Up, Housing and Communities (DLUHC) (2022) *Levelling Up the United Kingdom* (CP 604), at xiv. https://www.gov.uk/government/publications/levelling-up-the-united-kingdom

7 DLUHC (2022), at 3, see Reference 6.

8 Foundational Economy Collective (2022) *Foundational Economy. The Infrastructure of Everyday Life*, new ed. Manchester: Manchester University Press; Reeves R (2020) *The Everyday Economy*. https://www.rachelreevesmp.co.uk/wp-content/uploads/sites/96/2020/09/374425087-Rachel-Reeves-The-Everyday-Economy-1.pdf

9 Such as:

> the one village shop or pub, without which we are cut off from the essentials of a good life; childcare, which is not currently recognised as an essential plank of the country's infrastructure; and the buses and trains that connect us to apprenticeship and grandchildren, choices and chances.

Nandy L (2022) *All In: The Must-Read Manifesto for the Future of Britain*. Manchester: HarperNorth, p 147.

10 Create Streets Foundation (2023) *The Case for Place. Creating Prosperity Through the Economics of Attraction* (Report for Karbon Homes). https://www.karbonhomes.co.uk/media/16016/m01231a3-the-case-for-place-report-web-single-pages.pdf

11 Calafati L et al. (2023) *When Nothing Works. From Cost of Living to Foundational Liveability*. Manchester: Manchester University Press.

 https://doi.org/10.1080/2578711X.2023.2255004

Appendix: a timeline of Sacriston

1839	Sinking of Sacriston Colliery
1844	Opening of Church School
1854	Opening of Primitive Methodist Chapel
1857	Sacriston identified as a village for the first time on an Ordnance Survey map as a collection of terraces, two pubs (the Colliery Inn and the Boot and Shoe) and a Primitive Methodist Chapel
1863	Creation of Sacriston ecclesiastical parish
1866	Work begins on St Peter's, Church of England
1867	Catholic Mission established in Sacriston to minister to Irish immigrants
1869	Formation of the Durham Miner's Association
	Colliery acquired by Sir George Elliott, Bt and William Hunter
1871	First Durham Miners' Gala
1874	Formation of Sacriston Colliery Cricket Club
1877	Work begins on St Bede's Catholic Church. Completed 1881
1882	Opening of new Primitive Methodist Chapel
1884	Opening of St Bede's Catholic School
1894	Ownership of the colliery transferred to Charlaw & Sacriston Collieries, Company, Ltd. W. C. Blackett appointed Managing Director
1896	Charlaw and Sacriston Colliery Co. Ltd provides first street lighting in the village

https://doi.org/10.1080/2578711X.2023.2255008

1897	Opening of the Sacriston branch of the Annfield Plain Industrial and Cooperative Society
1898	Opening the Wesleyan Methodist Chapel
1902	Opening of the Sacriston Workmen's Club and Institute
1903	16 November. Two miners—hewers John Whittaker and Thomas McCormick—were killed as a result of an ingress of water. A third miner, Robert Richardson, was rescued after being trapped underground for four days. The rescue effort attracted national media attention. W. C. Blackett was among several who were awarded medals for bravery from the National Humane Society
1904	Opening of the Salvation Army Citadel
1906	John Wilkinson Taylor elected first Labour MP for Chester-le-Street, which includes Sacriston
1909	16 February. An explosion at nearby West Stanley Colliery killed 168 men and boys. W. C. Blackett led the rescue efforts and Sacriston miners were among the rescuers
	Opening of the County Council School on Witton Road
1914	*Kelly's Directory of Durham* lists over 80 commercial premises in the Sacriston and eight places of worship
	Outbreak of the First World War. Many Sacriston men enlist in the Durham Light Infantry and serve in the Tyneside Irish Battalions
1915	Committee established to provide support for Belgian refugees. Several families were housed in Sacriston during the war
1919	Labour takes control of Durham County Council, under the chairmanship of Peter Lee
	Jack Lawson (later Lord Lawson of Beamish) elected Labour MP for Chester-le-Street
1923	Opening of Sacriston Memorial Institute
	Roll of honour of was dead unveiled by W. C. Blackett
1925	Annie Errington elected to Chester-le-Street Rural District Council, one of the first women councillors in the country. She was appointed to the board of Chester-le-Street Poor Law Guardians
1926	General Strike and Lockout. Miners refuse to accept cuts to and extension of the working day and are locked out by the employers for seven months, causing immense hardship

	Durham Aged Mineworkers' Homes Association cottages opened in Sacriston
	Annie Errington visits Russia to speak in support of Durham miners and their industrial action
	Chester-le-Street Poor Guardians, including Annie Errington, surcharged and threatened with gaol for providing financial support to striking miners
1932	Opening of Fulforth Park
1936	Death of W. C. Blackett, Managing Director of Charlaw & Sacriston Collieries Co. Ltd
1938	Annie Errington is appointed Justice of the Peace
1939	Outbreak of the Second World War
1941	4 December. A fall of stone kills five miners at Sacriston Colliery: Joseph Welsh, 46; George W. Scott, 39; William Richardson, 50; and John William Britton, 47. At least 61 men died mining coal at Sacriston Colliery
1947	Nationalisation of the coal industry
1951	The 1951 Durham County Development Plan, anticipating the decline of the coal industry, classified all villages as an A–D settlement. In Category D, settlements for future development would be permitted, property demolished and the population relocated. A total of 114 settlements were placed in Category D in the 1951 Plan, rising to 121 in the revised Durham County Development Plan of 1964. No more than three had been completely demolished by 1968, but many were reduced in size. Sacriston was assigned to Category A, but nearby villages such as Edmondsley and Waldridge were assigned to Category D.
1961	Memorial Institute burned down
1964	Memorial Institute rebuilt and reopened
1966	Opening of Sacriston Secondary School (later Fyndoune School)
1971	Closure of the Sacriston branch of the Annfield Plain Industrial and Cooperative Society
1972	Miners' Strike
1974	Miners' Strike
1976	Demolition of Primitive Methodist Chapel
1979	Peak coal production at Sacriston Colliery
1981	First reported threat to close Sacriston Colliery

1984	6 March. Beginning of the Miner's Strike to oppose the National Coal Board's colliery closure plan
1985	3 March. End of Miners' Strike
	15 November. Closure of Sacriston Colliery
2006	Closure and deconsecration of St Peter's Church
2007	Work begins on a new community centre—the Fulforth Centre—to replace the Memorial Hall. Opened in 2008
2009	Memorial Hall demolished
2020	The Cooperative Buildings reopened as the Sacriston Enterprise Workshop
2021	Closure of Fyndoune School
	Labour loses control of Durham County Council for the first time in a century